FOOD
BUSINESS
SECRETS

Specialty Food Maker Reveals How to Reach
Six Figures in Sales with Retail and Farmers Markets.

FOOD BUSINESS
— SECRETS —

MICHAEL ADAMS

Table of Contents

Foreword by Brett Lindenberg, Founder of FoodTruckEmpire.com.

You picked up a copy of this book. This means you're thinking about taking your idea and turning it into a real food business. I want to commend you for taking the first key step in turning your vision into a real business.

The specialty food industry generates over $140 billion in annual revenue and is still growing. If you're thinking about producing an organic kale chip brand, taking your grandmother's raspberry jam recipe to the national level, or want to take your fudge to sell at the neighborhood farmer's market there's a big enough pie for all producers with a quality product to grab a slice of this demand.

There has never been an easier time to start a specialty food business either. There's a growing base of customers that want to support small producers like you with a story behind their brand. The logistics of getting food packaging designed and opportunities to market your business for free online with social media has never been easier. Thanks to cottage food laws, entrepreneurs across the United States can start a food business out of their home kitchen for minimal investment. More on these cottage food laws later in this guide.

But this doesn't mean you personally should start a food business. While this book shares the step-by-step process needed to get started there are also vivid stories from the front-lines included so you know what you're getting into.

It will take many hours and months of dedicated work to take a food product to retail and start generating sales. Ask yourself honestly... Is this something you will enjoy? If not, consider staying small so you can run the business on the side or on weekends at farmer's markets.

This book is not intended to steer you in any direction, but to give you the pros, cons, and what to expect in the real world.

With that being said, enjoy the process of starting and growing a business. There is nothing more fulfilling than taking an idea you dreamed up and making it a reality.

Before we get started, I encourage you to download our free Food Startup Business Kit here as a companion to this book: https://foodtruckempire.com/fbk-join/. We included templates and exclusive interviews with proven food entrepreneurs that supplement this guide and help you grow a food business.

Enjoy the guide! I wish success in your food startup!

Best,
Brett Lindenberg
Founder of FoodTruckEmpire.com

Part 1:
Launch Your Food Business

An actionable blue-print to help you take your food product everyone is raving about and build a profitable business. Since we are at the beginning, don't forget to download the free companion to this book the Food Business Startup Kit: https://foodtruckempire.com/fbk-join/. Inside you'll find business canvas templates, spreadsheets, and exclusive interviews to help you get started right.

Welcome!

This is day one. Day one of the most amazing transformations you'll go through. It's the first day of launching your food business. SO exciting! You're going to learn so much in this guide – and the others offered on the Gredio site. I'm excited to see where this course takes you and your food business.

What to Expect:

1. The focus is on you

This class is your time. It's your time to explore, learn, mull-it-over, and do what you need to do to build a successful food business. And I'm right there with you. If you have questions at any time, hop on a monthly webinar or send me a quick note.

2. Help is here

I'm not in this alone. I've taken twelve years of launching three food products and rolled it into one big knowledge ball for you to explore. It includes insights from family, friends, other food business owners, financial analysts, QuickBooks specialists, investors, line cooks, and more. And we're all here to help. Whether you're launching a side business or going at this full-throttle, help is closer than you think.

3. Use This Material as an Education Resource

While there are many books written on the subject, they're not actionable. You get the tools you need to build on your idea - not just read through a book and have no idea what to do! I'm all about results, so let's do this! Are you with me?

Course Overview:

- Are You Sure You Want to Do This?
- What to Do Before You Say "I Want to Start a Company!"
- Where to Produce Your Specialty Food Product
- How to Package Your Specialty Food Product
- Your First Jars - How to Be Awesome at Test Marketing
- Basic Financials: Determining the Cost of your Specialty Food Product

And a whole lot more -- that's just the beginning!

Before you start, you should stop

What? That doesn't make any sense. I know, but hear me out.

Many people get an idea in their head to start the most amazing food business ever. And they pour everything they've got into the business. That's not a bad thing, but it's not good either.

You start working 100 hour weeks. You miss your kid's soccer game, and your personal health starts to deteriorate. That's not what you thought would happen, is it?

And that's why you need to slow down.

Passion is best applied to a well-thought-out idea. When you put in long hours "building" your business, you skip over the fundamental reasons you're starting up.

If you're trying to generate some side-income or launch a food business as your retirement plan, your heart has to be in it. You need to love every minute of it. From the time you land your first retailer, to the time you're strapped for cash and your product gets recalled. Yes - the highs and the lows. You experience all of them as an entrepreneur - regardless of what business you're in.

So how do you know if your heart is in it?

I've started four companies and, at one point, my heart was in all of them. Even though your heart may be elsewhere, when you start your company, it's like a new child (except they don't throw up on you. Well, figuratively, they do!) While running these companies I arrived at three key principles that told me I was doing this for the right reasons. That my heart was in it.

 FOODTRUCKEMPIRE

1. You could pull an all-nighter and be excited the next morning

You shouldn't pull an all-nighter. That would just be crazy. But you should want to. There should be so much to do you could work through the night and be happy - even though you're running on jet fumes.

2. You can't stop talking to family and friends

Is a new idea in your head? Don't hide it from everyone. Your heart is in it when you can't stop telling people about your idea, how you've solved a business problem, or how cool your packaging is going to be.

3. You want to make a difference

Starting a food business is not about the money. It'll take a little bit of time for you to start moving some serious product. You should be in this for a different reason: sharing meals with the community, supporting other local producers, etc. If you're in it for reasons other than money, the cash will come.

This is how you should assess a new idea. Do you want to be doing this all night? Would you rather be doing something else?

Your criteria will be different. My heart is not your heart. You're motivated by different forces. Before you continue, make sure your heart is in it.

Remember, just because your parents, friends, and family think your spaghetti sauce is awesome doesn't mean you should go into business.

You have to want to go into business.

You can't stumble into business. It's a choice. In fact, it's your choice. And oftentimes, you'll be by yourself on this journey. Yes, you'll have the support of family and friends, but ultimately you're the one doing 99% of the work.

5 Things you probably didn't think about before saying YES to your food business

1. You need more cash than you think

It's possible to start your food business with just a couple hundred bucks, but as you produce more product, your cash demands increase. A couple hundred dollars turns into thousands in the blink of an eye. You're going to learn more about startup costs in a later lesson.

 FOODTRUCKEMPIRE

2. You need to dedicate your life to the business - including weekends

For seven months out of year, you're likely to never take a full weekend off. Why? Because store demos, farmer's markets and festivals happen on the weekends. It's a time when your customers are willing and able to purchase from you. This means you should be available!

3. You need to wear many hats

Chief cook and bottle washer isn't just a funny saying. Running your own food business means you do everything: manufacturing, accounting, cleanup, distribution, packaging, sales calls, hiring, firing, etc. Not until you get a bit bigger are you able to be off-responsibility to other vendors.

4. You need to make TONS of decisions

Not a big fan of making decisions? You better think about a new career path then. Owning a business is all about making decisions. Just like #3, you've got to decide everything. While it's good to have a mentor or someone to bounce ideas off of, you have the final say. Get used to picking 'yes' or 'no'.

5. You need to learn business - not just food production

What are you costs? What's your pricing model? How much do you make on a unit? What's your break even? What about your income statement? You need to know all of this - and don't just outsource it to an accountant. Get a grasp on your numbers.

Eye opening, isn't it? However, it should be inspiring, too. Starting a small food business is no easy feat. It takes several tons of dedication, perseverance, and planning. Simply popping up shop isn't recommended. I would imagine crashing and burning in a couple months isn't on your to-do list.

That's why you're getting actionable steps (some would call it homework) at the end of each of these segments.

Here's your homework for the first lesson:

Actionable Steps:

- Write a list of reasons why you want to start your food business. Is your heart in it?

Commit yourself to your business. Put your seatbelt on! It's going to be a crazy ride.

What to do before you start your food business

Did you do your homework? Are you ready to start your food business? If you are, read on. If not, take your time. Starting a business is a huge decision. It's a decision that can't be made in minutes. You need to sleep on it. Plus, these courses will always be here for you. They're not going anywhere!

Here's where you are:

- Are You Sure You Want to Do This?
- What to Do Before You Say "I Want to Start a Company!" **(your current class)**
- Where to Produce Your Specialty Food Product
- How to Package Your Specialty Food Product
- Your First Jars - How to Be Awesome at Test Marketing
- Basic Financials: Determining the Cost of your Specialty Food Product

Ready to rock and roll?

Ok - let's talk about the steps you should go through before you start your food business. It's not the most exciting part of being your own boss, but it needs to be done.

In the first class, you decided if your heart was in it. But that's just on an individual basis. Your business affects more than just you. It affects your family, especially spouse and children, your co-workers, and really anyone you come into contact with.

That means they're involved in the decision just as much as you are.

Talking through the decision with family and friends may bring up ideas you haven't even thought of, concerns you passed over, or best yet, praise for starting your own business.

These conversations (which I highly recommend you have) get touchy. Here's just a sampling of questions you might get grilled with:

- What about the time commitment?
- How much money do you hope to make?
- Do you want to do this full time?
- Where are you going to get the money to start?
- Why do you want to do this?
- Aren't there already thousands of (insert food here) available?
- You've never done this. Why now?

Sounds like an interrogation, doesn't it? Before you sit your spouse down on the couch, answer some of these questions - just scribble notes down in a notebook or type something up.

Tips for talking with your family and friends about your new venture:

1. Start talking about something else first

Don't you hate when others just come right out and say it? I do, too. That's why I think it's best to start talking about something else. Then ease yourself into the conversation you want to have.

2. Conversations are two ways

Make sure you're open to answering questions. Conversations are meant to be constructive and productive. Get your points across and then see if they've got any questions. If you don't have the answer, there's no shame in saying "I don't know."

3. They want to help you

Friends and family will chomp at the bit to help you out. And you should take their offer, even if you think it's going to be a headache. Why? Because you've got a million things on your plate. Wouldn't it be awesome if a couple were taken away?

4. Keep it to thirty minutes

Don't let the conversation drag. Assign a time limit. That way, if things blow up and you end up arguing, you can exit the conversation to take a breather.

5. Talk with multiple friends and family members

Don't just get one family member's opinion. Especially if they think you're out of your mind. Find a mix of those who give you constructive criticism and want to see you succeed. It's important to listen to criticism and praise. Your friends and family might bring up points you have yet to consider.

Don't be afraid to have these conversations right now. You're going to have them eventually, so get them out of the way, and let's move on to the next stop: Finding a mentor(s).

Next Step: Finding your mentor(s)

Oftentimes, it's great to find someone who knows what it's like to be in business. While they don't have to be a specialty food entrepreneur, find a local businessperson you respect.

 FOODTRUCKEMPIRE

Once you've got a short list (3 - 5 possible mentors), contact them to see if they'd be willing to help you out. Many of them will be more than willing to help you - and free of charge.

How are they able to help you for free?

Business people like to establish their own good will, credibility, and well, they like to help other people because they know what you're going through.

How to find a mentor:

1. Find the local business association

There's bound to be a business associate in almost every town. Do a quick Google search and locate yours. Attend some meetings and get to know the leadership. Then, ask if there's anyone in the association willing to help you out. You'll find a mentor pretty fast this way.

2. Work with your local SCORE chapter

This is a hidden secret. SCORE is a program started by the Small Business Administration to provide free help to local business owners. The best part? The counselors are local business people. Simply find a chapter, send in what you're looking for, and you'll get matched up in just a couple of days.

3. Take advantage of your network

You've been building a network ever since you could talk. It started with your parents, then your first group of friends, college friends, and so on. Tap your network to see who may be able to assist you as your business gets off the ground - and beyond.

While finding a mentor isn't mandatory, it's highly recommended. When you find someone wise beyond their years, you'll appreciate everything you learn from them.

Also, don't be afraid to switch mentors. Your needs change. Find a mentor who best fits your current situation.

Now that you've talked with family and friends and found a mentor, it's time to look inside yourself. To look for your vision. Here's more on why you (and I) need a vision:

I used to think visions were a pile of junk.

They didn't put me any closer to my goal of launching my own food products, figuring out price points, and selling at farmer's markets.

So, why did I also of a sudden know I needed a vision?

Turns out I needed a vision because you need to have a rough idea where your company is going. In 2013, I sat in on a lecture by Babson College professor, Michael Cummings, on entrepreneurial thought and action.

In addition to sparking several thoughts in my head, he also talked about having the 15-year, in-it-for-the-long-haul, determination and vision. Have a solid plan, but be prepared to pivot.

While I have a vision for this company, I figured it's more important for you as a specialty food business owner, to figure out your vision.

Is it world jam domination? **Do you want to be the best mustard in the midwest?** Or simply sell out of cookies every Saturday morning at the Farmer's Market?

Before you figure that out, I want to give you three tactics - or steps - I've used to come up with a vision - and you can use them too:

1. Figure out your non-money reason

What are you doing in business? If it's for the money, specialty food is not the best industry to be in. There's something else behind it - maybe community, your passion for cooking, or your desire to do something while the kids are away at school. Whatever it may be, arrive at your answer before you move on to steps 2 and 3.

2. Write 5 visions down

Just like your very first marmalade recipe, it's not going to be right. You have to taste-test and refine the recipe until you've arrived at something you're proud of; something that can drive your food business in the right direction.

3. Whittle to one and show your family

This is important for a couple of reasons. First it gets you in the habit of making decisions - of cutting options and to focus on doing one thing really well. If you're not 100% set on one vision, sleep on it and review it in the morning. With a fresh pair of eyes, you might like one better you crossed out the night before. Lastly, take your one vision and share it with your family.

Not only will they provide you with valuable feedback, they'll have a better idea of what you want to do and where you'd like to take the company. And I'd hope they back you 100%.

That's three quick steps to get you thinking about your vision. Whether you're just starting out or you're onto your third product line, a 10 or 15-year vision puts you on a path to success. How do you know it's the right path? You've just got to start walking.

 FOODTRUCKEMPIRE

With vision in hand, you're ready to get into the meat of launching your food company.

Next Step: Let's talk about research

Research has helped everyone, from Einstein to Mendel, and of course today's scientists. Now, it's going to help you. Doing research allows you to test the market, do your planning, and enter the market with a product that people not only love, but is priced right, and there's tremendous value.

Still not convinced? Here's three quick reasons why research will save your life:

1. Market size & number of competitors

There are some incredibly crowded markets in the specialty food industry (any condiment, jams, jellies, crackers, etc). But where you're going to initially focus for the first few years of your business is your local and regional area - not on a national scale. This means your research is going to be different than if you were planning a national product launch (which hopefully you're not right now!)

2. Your competitive advantage

"Everyone makes jam. What makes yours different?" You'll be able to answer this question when you do your research. Why? Because when you walk the aisles of your local grocer you know who your competitors are, what they're offering, and why your product is much more awesome.

3. Price

This is the most important research you can do. If you're pricing your product at $7.99 and the majority of your competition is several dollars less, you might be pricing yourself out of the market. And it's hard to justify that much value with many food products available today. You'll learn more about pricing later in this series.

Research shouldn't be boring. Every step of the way, you should have a smile on your face because your heart is in it. Right? If your heart isn't in it and you have no interest in doing research before you introduce your product, I'd recommend going back to the first class.

You're ready to research. What's the best way?

There are two types of market research to conduct before you even launch your product or go sell at a farmer's market:

- In-store research

- Online research

Let's tackle in-store research first because it's going to be the most critical to how you position your product in the market.

Before you get started, write down a list of every grocery store in your area. This could be 1, 5, or 10+ stores. After you've got a long list, circle the top five stores you want to see your product in.

Where would your product sell best? The best answer is probably where you shop. Why? Because you are likely to make products you would buy, your friends would buy, and others in your income bracket would purchase.

After you finish your list, move on to the 10 easy steps to in-store research below.

The 10 steps to easy in-store research

This is by no-means the gospel of research, but it will help you walk through your grocery store with a new set of eyes. (Side note: I do this for fun)

What you'll need:

- Notebook & pen (or fancy mobile device)
- Competitor's Worksheet
- An open mind - don't get discouraged!

1. Walk up and down every aisle

Go to the grocery store when you don't need groceries because you'll observe more. You won't be a good researcher if you're getting everything on your list heading out the door. Plus, when do you get an opportunity to go to the grocery store when you're not in a frenzy? Take this time to not only check out your competition but other products you might want to try.

2. Take note of what catches your eye and what you pick up

That leads to the next step. What catches your eye? In your product aisle and across the store? Is it the packaging? The unique flavors? The height of the product on the shelf? All of these factors combine to get you to pick up a product for a closer look. Take note of what you pick up and why.

3. Go to your competitive space (likely to be 4-8 feet of shelf space)

Now it's time to focus on your to-be product section. It's likely to be 4-8 feet of space - or two gondola sections. If it's spaghetti sauce, you might be looking at 12 feet of space.

 FOODTRUCKEMPIRE

4. Count the number of brands and products

Stand and count the number of brands and the size of their product line. Do the national brands have more products or do local brands prevail? This gives you an idea of the acceptance of locally-produced products in your market.

5. Write down information about local brands

Where are they located? Do they have a professional presence? How many products do they have? Get all the information down on your worksheet so you can use it to research online later.

6. Write down information for national brands

Do the same for national brands. While the answers may be similar, see if there are stark differences between ingredients used and packaging - there usually is.

7. Find the product you're most drawn to in your section

Why do this? Because you're likely to pick up your competitor's product - whether national or local. What do you like about it? Is it the flavor, the packaging? Make note of why you picked it up.

8. Ask an employee if they sell a lot of your chosen category

If you come across an employee stocking the shelves in your section, don't be afraid to ask questions. What are the popular brands? Has the shelf-stocker tried any of them? Many times the store employees are full of useful information to help you plan your product's introduction.

9. Purchase three of your competitors products (include national brands if you want)

Purchasing your competitor's products sounds crazy, right? Why should you support them? Well, it's good will initially, but you've got to taste your competition. You've got to make your product taste better. Is it creamy? Watery? Incredibly tasty? Keep an open mind. Obviously, you're going to think your products taste better, but your customers are going to bring up your competition in conversations. This means it's best to know what they taste like.

10. Note if cashier says anything about local products

When your bring your items up to the cashier (and it's not a self-checkout), see if they say anything about your purchases. Maybe they've tried them, just like the employee stocking the shelves. Remember, employees are full of knowledge.

Note: Retailers will notice you writing things down in a notebook. It's kind of hard not to. If you're asked to stop, stop and come back at a later time, make mental notes, or repeat this process at another store.

This research will shape where you position your company's products. Don't worry about fine-tuning your recipe, packaging, labeling, shelf-space, or manufacturing until you've done this step.

It's that crucial.

Let's move on to the next part of the research - the internet. Now, you can obviously waste all kinds of time scrolling through Facebook, looking at recipes on Pinterest, and finding funny videos to send to your friends.

That's why the internet portion is short, with three key things to find out. Plus, this research should be fun for you!

Internet research

Everyone knows how to Google search, so I won't go in-depth with this information, but I will give you a couple of tips to do the best internet research you can. Here's three key terms you should keep an eye out for:

1. Search for {Your Product} {Your Location} in Google

- Find Local Competition
- Read Their Stories
- Make Note of Their Product Diversity
- Do They Have an Online Presence?

2. Search broadly for {Your Product}

- Find National Competition
- Discover Similarities Between Successful Local Companies & National
- How Do They Engage Online?

3. Find Your State or Regional Association

- List of State Associations
- Networking Opportunity
- Observe Other Small Producers
- Think About Joining - it's a startup cost! (More on that below)

Of course you're free to keep exploring online, but be careful. Researching online could get you into a black hole. Wasting six hours on a Saturday researching online is not the best way to

move forward with starting your food business.

5 Mistakes to avoid when you start your business

It seems people are starting a food business almost every day. From jams and jellies, to prepared foods, and salad dressings - there's tons out there.

But some of them don't survive.

Some of them fail because they made critical mistakes in the very beginning. Here's a list of five things you may want to watch out for if you're thinking of starting a food business.

1. Not testing your concept on a smaller scale

I've been talking with many start-up food entrepreneurs who are adamant about going big right out the gate. Don't. Test your concept. Start with friends and family, move to a farmer's market, and then start getting your product in retailers around town. By starting small, you're able to prove your concept through test-marketing and not waste your precious cash.

2. Producing without a license or permit

The health inspector is like the local sheriff when it comes to food production. And you don't want to upset them! Why so important? Well, if you're caught in violation, the health inspector can shut you down right then and there.

Make sure you call the health department to see if you need a license to produce food - especially if you're thinking of producing food in your home. Licenses can cost anywhere from $50 - $500 and in some cases more. Make sure you budget for the cost, too.

3. Not knowing your product cost

Of any on this list, this is the most important. You have got to know how much it costs to produce your product. That means ingredients, packaging, and labor. (And even if you produce your product by yourself, there's still a labor cost!). Your product cost drives your company's profitability. If you're not charging enough for your food product, you're not going to be able to cover your operating costs.

4. Running out of cash in the first few months

Cash is king in any business. You need to hang onto it like your company depends on it. Because it does. If you're splurging on marketing you might not need or fancy labels, think about what that does to your product cost. Or, if you're buying supplies left and right, have you thought

 FOODTRUCKEMPIRE

about making them yourself? Oh, and not to mention cash for farmer's markets and producing your product. Make sure you have enough to keep you going - even when it's slow in the beginning.

5. Thinking you don't need help

You want to build your food business to the point where it's sustainable. You can put food on the table and a roof over your head. That would be awesome, right? The truth is you're going to need help to get there.

Analyze your business. Identify what you don't like to do. Then, find someone to do it for you. Yes, it costs money. But, what about avoiding burnout? You can't possibly do everything for ever. For example, I have my parents help out with shows, scheduling, hotels, and other logistics. (That's why my Mom's job title is the Conductor of Controlled Chaos - it's exactly what she does).

How to set up your business as a legal entity

Before we press on (and you get totally serious about this), it's important to get setup as a legal entity – the first step to becoming a real (holy cow - gasp) business.

When you're starting your business, one of the first things you need to think about is what kind of business you're going to start. You have lots of options:

- Sole proprietorship
- Cottage Food Business
- Limited Liability Company (LLC)
- S-corporation
- C-corporation
- Partnership
- Limited Liability Partnership (LLP)
- Benefit Corporation (B-Corp)
- Low profit LLC (L3C – Vermont specific)

See? Whoa. Overload. Just writing that list makes me anxious. As you navigate through these water's, I need to make one thing clear:

Do not file for a sole proprietorship.

Sole proprietorships are for people who work for themselves and their business is basically their name – freelancers, for example. The businesses' profit goes to one person and if you get sued, they go after your personal assets.

 FOODTRUCKEMPIRE

Cottage food business

You can start a food business that falls under the Cottage Food Laws. These are laws put in place so that small food producers can produce food inside their home kitchen and sell it. This is an incredible low-cost way to get started in the food business and test your concept with extremely little risk from a financial perspective.

Each state has a different cottage food business laws and there are restrictions on what foods can be produced and sold under this designation. Lower risk foods like popcorn, fudge, jelly, and many other foods can be safely produced. Food products like custard that is made with eggs is often not allowed because there's a higher risk of contamination from salmonella.

There are also annual income restrictions that vary widely by state. In California for example you can sell well over $50,000 annually. In Florida, you can sell less than $30,000 annually. To get up-to-speed on your states rules check out: https://forrager.com/laws/.

If you want to get started on a budget to prove market fit this is a fantastic option. As your food brand grows due to increased sales you can move on to one of the entities listed below.

Enter the Limited Liability Corporation (LLC).

The beauty with an LLC is you get all the liability (hence, why it's limited) taken off of you. That means when someone goes to sue you, it's against the company and its assets (or lack thereof). One downside: If you make your LLC a pass-through entity, meaning all profits go on a personal income statement, you actually get taxed twice. Once for the company and a second time for self-employment tax (15.3%). Many food companies register as a LLC when they're starting out.

Getting taxed twice is a bummer though.

Enter the Corporation (S-corp and C-corp).

Corporations operate as their own entity. So, basically you get paid a salary and get taxed on that income only – not the income of your business. And there's a difference between an S-corp and a C-corp – it's crucial for your business.

The other types of business formations are much smaller. I recommend you choose an LLC or an S-corp/C-corp.

The SBA has a great resource for choosing your business formation.

How to file your business formation: Generally, it happens at the Secretary of State's Office online. You can file online and find if your name is already taken by another person.

If you start an LLC and it isn't the name of the business, you'll want to file a DBA – that's Doing Business As – which represents your business publicly.

Other paperwork you want to get:

The Small Business Administration has a list of everything you need to start your business. Click here to view the list.

Get a rough idea of startup costs

Almost done! After getting yourself on board, listening to feedback from family and friends, as well as doing basic industry research, you've ready for the final step to see if you've got everything lined up to get started with your food business: money.

Money is a tough subject

Every time financials come up, you're bound for a super headache. Finding startup funds is not the same as making delicious food, so I'll make this quick and painless for you.

Before I get too deep, I want to bring something up.

For some of you, money may be a touchy subject - especially if you've got to put a roof over your head and food on the table for your family. That requires a certain amount of cash and then you have to find a way to fund your business. But, starting a food business doesn't mean millions of dollars to fit up a brand-new kitchen. It's doable with a couple of thousand dollars - or even a couple hundred if you're thrifty.

The best way to explain startups is to compare the three food companies I've started. This gives you a better idea of how to fund your own companies.

In my own experience

I started three food companies - and all three were completely different financial strategies. Here's how they all played out:

1st Company: Adams' Cookie House

I was 15 when I started my first company selling chocolate chip cookies on Fridays in front of a hair salon in town. I got the money for my first few batches from my parents. I didn't get an allowance, so there wasn't too much money to my name.

2nd Company: Eddie's Energy Bars

Two years later, I launched an energy bar company. This time, I had enough money from working retail during high school to start this company. It was self-funded for 3.5 years and I never took a loan.

3rd Company: Green Mountain Mustard

The money I earned from Eddie's Energy Bars went into Green Mountain Mustard, so you could say this was self-funded as well.

As you can see, my three food businesses were self-funded. (What bank is going to loan a 17 year-old kid money these days?). That means food businesses don't take too much to get up and running, right? Maybe. Here's a quick breakdown of what you'll need to get going:

What do I need to get started?

Honestly, not that much. Here's a short (not all-inclusive) list:

- Food Licenses ($100-$500) ← don't skip these!
- State Business Registration Fees ($100)
- Opening a Bank Account ($50)
- Product Liability Insurance ($500-$1,000/year)
- Recipe Process Approval ($70-$100/recipe)
- Ingredients
- Labels and Packaging
- Kitchen Tools & Equipment (misc)
- Website ($1,000)
- Business cards ($50)
- Sales sheets ($20)

How much money does a typical food business spend to start-up?

I priced a couple of things out above. For my three companies, I started with $50, $300, and $4,000. And believe me, was I cheap. I only did what I needed to do. As I grew I got insurance, process approvals and such. But to test if I had a product people loved, it didn't cost too much.

If I had to throw a ball-park price for starting your food company, I'd go with $3,000 - $5,000. This assumes you pay a college student to help you design packaging and your website. It also assumes you have limited equipment needs.

Should you need to invest in your own kitchen, this number is going to be significantly higher.

 FOODTRUCKEMPIRE

Should you start for less?

You don't need all the bells and whistles. Hold off on the fancy packaging design until you get some cash - or do it yourself. I would absolutely get your licenses and fees in-line. That's a non-negotiable. Everything else is up to you: buy used equipment, get template business cards, etc.

With a (very) rough idea of start-up costs, you're probably wondering where the money is going to come from. Let's take a look at several ways you could secure your startup capital.

Where to find your start-up capital

1. Self-funded

While I don't have the stats, I would bet this is how the majority of small food businesses are started. Using cash from your checking account (or shared account if you're married) is easy and quick.

2. Bank loan

Only do this if you need to purchase a large piece of equipment to get your production started. The bank will likely want you to have some skin in the game. Be prepared to put 20-30% of your cash down before the bank will even look at your application.

3. Credit card

Have you read the stories about food businesses launching on three - five credit cards? Yep - it's true. And it's financially risky. Credit cards carry high interest rates and you may not be able to pay them off on time. If you can, avoid this funding source.

4. Friends and family

Your food business could definitely get launched with a small loan from family and friends. They're more likely to give you $5,000 than $50,000. A couple words of wisdom: write up a contract, pay your friend interest, and write a one-page business plan.

5. Use Kickstarter (or another crowd-funding source)

Kickstarter allows you to publish your idea to the masses with a quick video. Then, friends can invest as little as a $1 in your fledgling venture. The catch? If you don't reach your fundraising goal, you don't get any of the money raised.

5. Savings/401K

This is the personally-funded part. If you've got the money in your checking or savings account, this is the best way to get your food business started. Why? You don't have to pay anyone back but yourself!

6. SBA loan or micro-loan

The Small Business Administration is on your side. And so are the local economic groups by you. Look at the eligibility requirements before you apply to make sure you qualify. These loan programs may require a bit more planning, but it'll be worth it when you start to run your business.

7. Business plan competition

Relatively new to the scene, business plan competitions are a great way to not only get exposure for your idea, but get some serious cash if you win. Many business plan competitions have at least $5,000 up for grabs. And if you don't win, there may be someone in the audience interested in giving your company a shot.

Getting cash to start your business can be a challenging hurdle to jump. Hopefully with these seven ways, you'll have plenty of options to get going. If you're struggling, don't give up. Once you get past the question of how you're going to fund your company, it'll be a huge weight lifted off your food business chest.

Pro Tip: Don't Waste Your Money Until Your Business Plan and Product Strategy Are in Place. Poorly spent business funds are a big reason business go out of business

8. Kiva.org

This is a non-profit organization that helps small businesses get loans. They help small food producers get access to capital all the time all around the world. There is a limit to the size of that loan you get through this platform (around $15,000 but check their website for the latest figures). Unlike traditional lenders, they don't check credit scores either so this can be a good option for folks with little or no credit.

Here's your homework for the second lesson:

Actionable steps:

- Talk with the family affected by your new business. Make sure they're on board.

- Start thinking about who your entrepreneurial mentor could be.

- Get started with in-store and online research (this process is ongoing)

- Write down basic start-up costs for your food-business

Worksheets

- Mentor Brainstorming Worksheet

- In-Store Research Worksheet

- Online Research Worksheet

- Estimated Startup Costs Worksheet

- Business Plan Template

How-to guide: printing labels for your food business

In June 2010, I produced my first large run with a co-packer. It went smoothly until I determined the net weight on my labels was not the actual net weight of what was in the jar.

Fail.

That's what inspired me to write today's post — all about food labeling requirements. What goes on your food label is one of the most complex tasks to complete when you're starting your food business. There are legal requirements, font size requirements, weights, and more. Just grab the Excedrin bottle. Seriously.

That's why it's all sorted out for you right here, right now. Let's get started:

There are three parts to your label:

1. Principal display panel – the part that faces the customer when your product is on the shelf

2. Right display panel – to the right of your principal display panel

3. Left display panel – to the left of your principal display panel

Let's start with the principal display panel.

What goes on your principal display panel?

Company name & logo: this can be any size and color, but it needs to be identifiable because consumers have to find it on the shelf. When I was first starting out, our logo was huge — half the height of the jar. Then, when we redesigned our labels, it got much smaller. That's because we wanted our product names (which are remembered by our customers) to steal the show. It's different for every company, so make sure your brand is recognizable.

Product name: Does your product have a fun name like my mustards? Or do you simply want to say Horseradish, Peach Ginger, or Hot & Spicy? Describe your product, then identify it (see below).

Product identification: What do you sell? Even though you think it's obvious, you've got to explain what it is? Is it cookies, brownies, mustard, salad dressing, bbq sauce, etc. Don't leave the contents of your bottle up to your consumer to figure out.

Product claims: Vegan, gluten free, non-gmo, organic, etc. What claims is your product making? Do you have documentation to prove your claims? Do not lie. Customers trust you when they purchase their product. If you lose their trust, you lose business. These can also go on the sides of your packaging, but consumers don't typically rotate the product. That means you've got to shout it from the rooftops on the front of your label.

Net weight: Just because you have an 8-ounce jar doesn't mean 8 ounces of product goes in it. For example, water is not the same weight as concrete. Get your net weight right so that you can weigh your filled product to make sure there's enough sauce in the jar. Yes, you can be over by a couple grams, but don't be under. That's illegal because you're deceiving the customer. You can find your net weight by filling your container and weighing it. Then, weigh an empty container. Subtract the two numbers and you've got your net weight? Try to keep it to a nice round number – 9 oz, 3.5 oz. Makes the per ounce (or gram) calculations easier for retailers and customers.

What goes on your right display panel?

Nutrition facts and ingredient statement

Place of manufacture: Who are you and where do you make this product? Include full company name, town, state, and zip code. You can include your street address if you'd like love letters, but it's not required (**some states it is required). Use your home address or your "warehouse".

Phone number: Smart to include here if people have questions. We used to put our home number but that quickly got annoying. On our next reprint, we switched to a free Google Voice

phone number. It's amazing. Just get one to have it. You can screen calls, listen & archive voicemail anywhere, and the calls can go straight to your cell phone if you'd like. Another example is Grasshopper if you have a small team and want to have that "office" feel.

UPC Code (this can also go on your left display panel): There's been a lot of talk about using recycled barcodes. Don't do it. Yes, it's cheaper. But, if you want to get into large grocery stores, they require your GS1 prefix (which isn't unique to you if you buy recycled barcodes). Bite the bullet and register with the GS1. Up to 100 barcodes have a startup fee of $750 plus an annual renewal of $150. Get more information on how to get a barcode for your food product.

What goes on your left display panel?

Your left display panel is pretty much a blank canvas. But here are a couple things you can add to make it a bit more interesting.

How to use your product: When your product is on the shelf, the normal consumer has no idea what to do with it, or that you have these magical ways to use it. Let them know about recipe ideas, your personal favorites, and how they might actually use the whole jar or package and buy more – Yes – MORE!

Your company story: Who makes the stuff? Why'd you start your company? Are you super-tiny? Let customers experience your company in a few words. And entice them to learn more by visiting your website. And pictures of the founders – or signatures – are a great personal touch.

Product claims: If you'd like to expand on your product claims or mention how you source ingredients, let your customers know. They'll appreciate your honesty. Remember, lying doesn't get you anywhere in the food business.

Social media: Are you on facebook, twitter, instagram, and pinterest? Put logos on your packaging or list your social media addresses. I personally just do the icons. And only put accounts you're most active on. That way, when customers view your dead twitter account they aren't turned off when the last update is from three years ago. And your profile picture is still an egg. And QR codes? Don't do it. They're ugly. And people aren't going to whip out their smartphone to scan your code that goes to your website. That's not useful to them.

Now, that you've got all the information, you may be wondering how this all comes together into something that doesn't look like you made it in Microsoft paint? (PSA: don't make your label in paint, MS word, or the like use Canva.com instead).

 FOODTRUCKEMPIRE

How to make your first label:

When I was starting out (technically way back in 2007 at a farmer's market) I used ball jars from Wal-Mart and two address labels. The front label had my logo (Green Mountain Mustard). The back label had ingredients, town, and phone number. Illegal? You betcha. There was no net weight. Didn't even know I needed one. It worked for the time being.

If you're just starting out, printing labels off of your computer is perfectly fine.

I did for the first two years. I designed something in Adobe Photoshop. If you don't have photoshop, use Microsoft Word. Even though I despise doing anything in Microsoft word now, it's actually quite easy:

1. Find the label you want. There are thousands of sizes, colors, textures, waterproof, etc. The best play to buy labels online isOnlineLabels.com — way cheaper than Staples or Office Depot.

2. Download the corresponding template. Most labels correspond to an Avery design template. You can download label templates here. They come in either PDF or Microsoft Word formats. Open the file and get to work.

3. Design your label. There are a couple ways to do this. You can design your label in Microsoft Word using the text tools, colors, and clip art (not recommended) or you can import your logo and use the same text to format ingredients and all the other label requirements. Keep the same color scheme across your product line so it looks put together – even though you're printing them on your home computer. Speaking of printing....

4. Print your labels. Simply go to file > print and fire away. It sounds simple, but printing is actually a bit more complex. First thing to determine is what kind of printer you have. Any inkjet printer will print labels at lower quality. They'll also run and smudge if they get wet (That's happened to me before, and it's ugly). So much for giving your product as a gift, huh? The other kind of printer is a color laser printer.

This prints higher quality – and higher resolution – labels. You can pick one up for a couple hundred bucks. It's a great investment if you're just getting started.

Now that I've covered printing your own labels, you may be thinking, ok – get to the good stuff. How do I go about getting legit labels? Like grocery-store-worthy labels? Here we go.

How to get your labels professionally printed:

So you're selling enough product that your labels could be professionally printed? For me, that mark was comfortably being able to use at least 1,000 labels a month. Then, I could order in bulk to get my cost own with the printer. Why wait? Well, getting your labels printed can be

expensive. Even if you go with an online vendor with "great prices" it can be expensive. So, let's start with finding a label printer.

How to find a label printing company

1. Look locally

Simply search for "label printing company" and there's bound to be a couple within 50-100 miles. Call them up, go see their facility, and meet the sales and production teams. Shaking the hand of the production manager at the company we use was definitely reassuring. (Ok, I'm a sucker for working with local companies).

2. Search for online providers

There are tons of online providers of label printing. Most work on high margins and charge accordingly. Price it out, shop around, and find the best price. Ask for a sample kit of different sizes, shapes, and materials. That way, you'll be better educated when you talk to them on the phone about what you're looking to do. Pro tip: don't place the order blind. Pick up the phone. Save money – and your next headache.

3. Ask around

I found my current printer through personal relationships (see below), but my first print contact came from another food producer. I loved their labels and asked where they got them printed.

Just like searching for an ingredient supplier or a finding a co-packer, there are certain questions you should ask to find the perfect label partner for your food business:

What kind of printer do you have?

This is important because it determines your printer's capabilities. Do they print digitally? Flexographically? Boxes, labels, bags, etc? Some printers print more labels per hour which reduces your cost, but the printer's overhead. That may ultimately mean a higher price, but only calling will find the answer for you.

How many labels do you need?

I print 20-40k labels at a time. With that being said, I've also had to trash labels multiple times because of spelling errors, name-changes, or rebranding my food business. Most label printers have label minimums as low as 100. But you'll pay a pretty penny. Once you get into several thousand labels, you'll see a nice price break. Then, the difference between say, 60,000 and 80,000 labels is negligible.

 FOODTRUCKEMPIRE

How much are start-up costs for brand-new label designs?

There may be art design fees, printing plate costs (only if you're printing flexographically) and setup fees. Plus shipping and other miscellaneous fees. Make sure these are calculated into your per unit labels cost and ultimately your food product cost.

What's your lead time for an order?

Don't run out of labels. I've done it several times and it's not exciting. Especially if you use a co-packer. Then, you end up labeling yourself and it takes hours because you don't have access to a machine (we still don't :p). Plan ahead – a couple weeks – for ordering more labels. That way, you'll have plenty for your next production.

Who else do you print labels for?

Testimonials are the best form of marketing for any label printer (like the one below I wrote for Creative Labels of Vermont). Ask who else they print labels for, send them an email and ask about their experience, possible pricing, and if they have had any problems. If not, get a quote and start your own relationship. Plus, the list of their clients is a major source of credibility.

Will you help me through the label purchase process?

I get more into customer relationships below, but if you're a first-timer, label printing is straight-up daunting. You want to work with account managers who walk you through each step – from design to final printing. Because you don't need to worry about it anymore. Your label printer does. Make sure you've got a great team to work with.

These questions, while obvious, are the ones you've got to ask. Many times, label printers are the "you get what you pay for" type. The best price doesn't always mean the best quality. And quality is important. Your label is your first interaction you have with your customer on a store shelf. It shouldn't look like crap, right? Right.

What you need to decide about your labels:

1. Size / How many

How big do you want your labels? Should they cover the whole container? Do you want a top and bottom label? A top label and a wrap-around label. Keep in mind, the more labels you use, the higher your costs become.

2. Shape

Rectangular? Rounded corners? Or how about a die-cut? A die-cut is a special shape that you pay extra for up-front. It could be an outline around a character, bubble shape, or hole in your

label to show your product inside its container. Die- cuts make your product stand-out on the shelf and create a powerful brand message.

3. Number of Colors

A black and white label is the least expensive. As you start adding colors – or printing full color – the cost goes up. Think about this when designing your labels. One way to save money on label printing is to keep your design the same and only change certain characteristics. That way you avoid multiple plate charges and switch-overs (the time it takes from switch to printing another design).

4. Material

It's mind-blowing to learn how many kinds of labels there are. There are solid color, white, textured (like wine labels), clear, thick, thin, UV coated (doesn't deteriorate in light), matte, gloss, foil-printed. Craziness. Let your account manager know about what you're putting the label on – the material, the temperature you fill your product, and what you'd like it to look like when it (maybe) goes in the fridge – no runny labels! This is where a sample pack is helpful. It allows you to see your printer's capabilities and select the best material for your project.

5. Quantity

Quantity plays a big role in price. Every penny counts when you're talking about product cost. That means if you can order thousands of labels, do it. Your price drops significantly – to the tune of 7 to 10 cents or more. I have ordered for the entire year at once and it's been a good strategy. If you think you're going to make changes to your labels, order less so you're not stuck with old labels. They'll just be piles of money in your basement.

A note about relationship building and customer service:

Even after all the questions get asked and the order gets processed, you want a relationship with your printer. They are a crucial partner to your success. Know who to talk to, chat with them at events. Why? They know everyone who is everyone in the local food scene. And I mean everyone. They're connected like good wifi. For real. Relationship is the reason I switched printers.

Why I switched printers:

In 2010, I started with a company out of NY. I switched to them because of the price. And we all know price isn't the only reason we buy from people. But, they were inexpensive. Until the quality dropped and they were unable to print my newly labeled designs (you know the ones I almost lost $2,000 printing?).

I was in a time crunch. The labels needed to be printed, like, yesterday.

That's when I remembered (ages ago) speaking with Zara from Creative Labels of Vermont (our current printer). She had been trying to win my business ever since the first jar of Green Mountain Mustard hit the shelf. And she won it in minutes after I contacted her in a bind.

"I need these labels rushed. My current printer says it's impossible to print but I don't believe him. Get it done by Friday and you've got my business."

Within minutes, she not only said it was definitely possible, but she came back with a price I couldn't turn down. The artwork was sent over and our labels were ready to print. At 6:30pm the night before printing, I forgot the "refrigerate after opening". After basically suffering a mini heart attack, it was fixed at no additional cost. Seriously.

Not only that, I was able to see the press proof the morning of – an actual label in my hands – for free. They're 10 minutes away from my kitchen, so I save on shipping costs, too — but bottom line: Zara at Creative Labels of Vermont has done an amazing job of making me feel comfortable through the entire process, connecting me with tons of other start-up food producers, and investing in our relationship – regardless of how super-tiny my orders are.

Conclusion:

Labels are time consuming to figure out. That's why, when you reach the point where you need to get labels printed, you should invest time into finding the right printer for your needs – even if it means making the switch to another provider.

I urge you to find a label printer with an eye on relationship building who has the same passion for making your product beautiful on the shelf. It's vital to the success of your business.

5 Things to do before you send your labels to print:

1. Send them to 3 different people who have never seen them

Whenever I'm spending thousands of dollars on printed materials – whether a postcard, recipe sheet, or labels – I have multiple people look them over. That way, your grammatical errors will (hopefully) get caught, and poor word choices will be replaced with better word choices. Have family and friends look them over to make sure everything is good to go.

2. Make sure your barcodes scan at retail

Before sending labels off to the printer, I printed a sheet of barcodes, drove to my local grocery store (I did this at an independently owned store) and asked them to scan the barcodes to make sure everything scanned correctly. While it won't show up in their system (unless it's a matching code), you'll known in seconds whether or not you need to change the size of the barcode. We

cut our barcode height in half to save room for the nutrition panel, so we wanted to make sure the product would scan.

3. Decide on your label material – get samples

When you're getting quotes from label companies, ask for samples. Don't just say you want some labels. They could be paper, matte, glossy, UV-coated, full-color, black and white, thermal, digital, flexographic. There's a million different solutions to label your product. Have a conversation with the account manager to determine the label that's best for your product.

4. Follow the FDA guidelines – if you have questions ask

There's a lot required of your company when you want to take the next step beyond just selling at bake sales or to family and friends. Here's just a couple requirements: business name, place of business, ingredient statement, net weight, and more. Nutrition facts aren't required (although highly recommended), until you are producing over 100,000 units of a product.

5. Print out labels and put them on jars. Then, put them on a shelf.

Hopefully you have a printer because you'll need it to print out mock labels. When I was working with my design team, I initially looked at my designs on the computer. That led me to choose one design over another. Then I printed them out. The design I originally loved on the computer was immediately thrown out. Putting your labels on your jars and throwing them on a mantle or bookshelf is important because it gives you an idea of what your new label may look like on the retail shelf. Sure, it won't be print-quality, but you'll have a good idea.

Besides glass, labels are one of the most expensive investments you're going to make starting your own food company. It's crucial to get it right the first time so you don't waste thousands of dollars getting them re-printed.

**Disclaimer: Please use this advice as guidance to creating and printing your food labels. Consult your Agency on Agriculture & Markets to get your labels approved by your state authority before printing.

Where to produce your specialty food product

You're starting to ramp up now!

Hopefully you had some time to talk with family and friends about your new food business. Remember, if there was a lot of tough love going around, keep your head up. There will always be naysayers telling you that you won't be able to do it. It's your business. Your determination and drive will help you succeed.

And that's also what your mentor is for. Have you found one yet? If not, don't wait too long. When the going gets tough, you'll want your mentor there to help you through the hard times.

And lastly how did the research and startup planning go? Do you have a lot of competition or a wide open market?

Let's get started with your third class: Where to Produce Your Product

This is the number one question I get when entrepreneurs ask me about starting their own company: Where do you produce your product?

Depending on where you're located, the question can be answered pretty simply - or it can be incredibly complicated (and unfortunately expensive).

There are 3 options to produce your product:

- Produce in your home (an option for some of you)
- Produce in a commercial kitchen
- Produce with a co-packer (in a commercial kitchen)

Over the next several pages, you'll learn the pros and cons of each production space, stories from producers who are in each situation and why they chose that route. Also, we'll dabble in some legality with each situation to make sure your company is covered.

Option #1: Producing in your home

At first glance, you figure you'll produce in your house. It'll be cheap, you get to stay home with the kids, and everything will be perfect.

Well - not exactly.

Many states don't allow you to produce commercially-available products in your home kitchen. That means you can't sell the hot fudge sauce you made on your stove-top to the store in town. It's illegal.

How do I know if I can make and sell products produced in my home?

Your state needs to have a cottage food law. This means you're able to get started in your home and sell at farmer's markets and maybe in retailers - every state is different. Luckily, there's a list of states with cottage food laws, thanks to CottageFoodLaws.com. See if your state is on the list and read up on the law.

Why isn't my state on that list?

Not every state has a cottage food law. It's a bummer, but you can write to your local representative to consider a cottage food law. In the meantime, you'll need to find another way to produce your product. And that's what options 2 - 4 are for.

Before we move on, I want to get pros and cons out of the way for you. If you want to skip down to more information about producing in your home, by all means, go for it.

11 reasons to start a home-based food business:

1. Low overhead costs

When you bake and produce at home, you have less costs: no rent, a slight rise in utilities, and no employees to manage. That saves you a ton of money when you're up and running.

2. The kitchen is always open

Struggling to find kitchen time locally? That's not a problem when you produce in your home. Whether you like to bake scones at 3am or do large BBQ sauce runs at 8:30pm, the choice is yours. Your home kitchen is always open.

3. You have no commute

A lot of food producers commute over 90 minutes to their shared-use kitchen. Not only do they spend a lot of money on gas, it's hard to drive and grow your food business at the same time. Lucky for you, your commute from your bed to the mixer is probably 60 seconds (and you can pick up a fresh-baked scone along the way).

4. Plenty of storage

Unless you live in a studio or one-bedroom apartment, chances are you've got some extra space to store everything. In many commercial kitchens, pallet storage costs a lot of money. Thankfully, you've got a spare bedroom to store cases upon cases of your finished product. And your basement can become storage for your ingredients.

5. You know your way around your kitchen

Large commercial kitchens are daunting. Almost everything is stainless steel, you're not familiar with the equipment, and you need to go through orientation just to learn the ropes. When you

 FOODTRUCKEMPIRE

work in your own kitchen, you know where everything is. This means you make more product faster and cut down on your labor costs.

6. Get your kids involved

If you're a stay-at-home Mom, you can get your little helpers involved in your food business. Maybe they can help get the sugar or drop cookies onto a baking sheet. Getting your kids' hands dirty with cooking and baking is a great way to plant the foodie seed early and watch them develop into culinary super-heroes!

7. Have friends over for taste-testing parties

When you're known as the cook or baker, friends ever-so-casually invite themselves over. Now, you have an opportunity to have them test your food products. (Of course, many of your taste-testers shouldn't be friends and family).

8. Less legal red tape

Commercial kitchens have to go through a laundry list of certifications - especially if they have to be certified gluten-free, kosher, or organic. (Plus, the certifications cost thousands of dollars). Producing in your home likely comes with a small license fee and a revenue cap you have to stay below. Call your local health department to find out more.

9. Get closer to your family

Starting your business is a great way to bring the whole family together. As I stated in reason 6, you've already got your kids involved. Take family time to sell your wares at farmer's markets, craft fairs, and local retailers. Give each family member a job. That way you've really got a family business!

10. Make what you love

I'm sure you've read a lot about doing what you love, but what about making what you love? For food business owners, loving what you're making is an ingredient for success. The second you hate doing what you're doing, it's time to find another home-based business.

11. Opportunity to test the waters

Launch your food business - just do it. Today sounds good. The sum of these benefits is that there's no better time to get started than right now. See what happens because you never know. Start selling your hot sauce. Bake your first batch of brownies. Get out there and build an amazing home-based food business.

There you have it. 11 reasons to fire up your oven, get the mixer out and start your company.

But it's not all chocolate chip cookies and carrot cake. Let's look at some of the reasons not to start your own business.

5 reasons not to start a home-based food business

1. It's a strain on your relationships

Just like it can help bring the family closer, a home-based food business can also tear the family apart. When your kitchen is full of 50# bags of oats, your spare bedroom has a gazillion plastic containers, and no longer have an air-hockey table in the basement, it can cause friction between your kids, spouse, and you. Make sure to set boundaries as to how your business impacts your family-life. Remember, work-life balance is important.

2. You think you make a great product

A lot of home-based chefs and food producers start companies because they want to. Unfortunately, they haven't done their test marketing. People might not buy your product at the price you're asking. This means you've got to do your research and make sure you're set up for success.

3. You may not have the space

I know plenty of entrepreneurs who rent storage lockers to store finished product because they don't have room in their homes. Plan out where everything is going to go and make sure you have the space. If not, you might want to scale back your empire.

4. Producing a recipe in larger quantities

Making one banana cream pie is a lot different than making twelve of them. Scaling your recipes can be a challenge and you might not get it right the first time (it's happened to me plenty of times). Things like taste, texture, and appearance start to change when you produce a lot of products.

5. Time and energy demand

Let's face it - it takes a lot of energy to keep pushing through the ups and downs of owning a food business. Do you have the time to devote to starting your own food business? Remember, you don't just make the product - you package it, label it, sell it, do the accounting, clean the kitchen, etc. It's a lot of work. Are you ready?

Starting a home-based food business can be a launching pad to something bigger. My first two food companies started in my parent's house. There were ups and downs, of course, but it was a fun experience.

Let's assume you can produce in your home

Before you go on, read this: Producing in your home should be taken seriously. You're not baking a cake for the bake sale at your daughter's school. You're selling products for public consumption. That means no licking the bowl, no letting your dog jump on the counter, and no carelessness in washing your equipment.

Step 1: Investigate state laws

This means calling your local health department. You can find your local health department's contact information here.

Every state law is different. In Vermont, for example, if you produce a baked product, you can be licensed as a home bakery for $50/year. If you produce a processed product (condiments, sauces, etc) you can produce in your home if you have less than $10,000 in gross sales. Over $10,000 in revenue? That's when you need a health inspection of your house (or production facility). And the inspectors take their job seriously! Not to mention the $125 annual license fee.

REMINDER: It's different for every state, so get in touch with your state's health department. If you need to be inspected, do it. The health department has the power to shut you down immediately (and if you own a chocolate company, that could be pretty upsetting for your customers).

Step 2: Prepare for certification

This shouldn't take too long if you're getting your home certified as a bakery or production area. From my experience they'll check the following:

- Flooring, Paint, and Overall Appearance of Production Area
- Food Product Labeling (more on that in a later class)
- Your Refrigerator and Freezer temperatures (basically, make sure they're cold enough)

Clean down all surfaces using natural (non-chemical) cleaners and use brown bio- degradable paper towels. Store your company ingredients separately from your personal things, and make sure everything is in a labeled food-grade container. Place ingredients off the floor on shelving (or kitchen cabinets).

 FOODTRUCKEMPIRE

The inspector will look over your space and make notes on their inspection sheet. Don't freak out and answer all questions truthfully. Keep a record of your inspection and your license on you - and in the kitchen - at all times.

Bonus tip: Health inspectors are known for surprise inspections, so keep your kitchen in tip-top shape.

Step 3: Get your recipe(s) approved

For all processed products like condiments, sauces, jams, jellies, you need a "scheduled process". If you have a bakery item, you do not need to fill this form out.

What's a scheduled process?

A scheduled process is something you submit to a process authority (food scientist) that details how you make your product. They approve it to be commercially produced.

What's included in a scheduled process?

You've got basic company information, recipe name, list of ingredients, detailed process, pH, aW (water activity), container type and size, as well as how you plan to sell the product

Why do I need this?

This is like the "seal of approval for your recipe". It's what you follow every time you make your recipe because it's the approved process.

How do I fill one out?

It's super simple. Here's a link to the Cornell Food Lab's: https://cfvc.foodscience.cals.cornell.edu/getting-started/. I recommend the Cornell Food Lab because their turnaround is quick (4-6 weeks) and I've never run into any problems. NC State, the University of Maine, and Nebraska have food science departments, too.

Why do I have to weigh everything out?

You'll notice every ingredient needs to be weighed out. That's because a cup of molasses is not the same weight as a cup of salt. The volume is drastically different. Take the time to weigh everything out because it will help with recipe scaling later down the road. Plus, if you have someone co-pack your product, they'll want your recipe in weight measurements.

How much does it cost?

The Cornell Food Lab charges $95 a recipe. Yep - it's not cheap, but get it done before you start producing large amounts of product and the production process will go a lot smoother.

 **FOODTRUCK**EMPIRE

This is, in effect, your intellectual property. Getting your recipes approved means your business has value. If and when you sell, the buyer is going to want scheduled process documents to show your recipes have been verified by food scientists and are safe to manufacture.

With your recipes completed and approved, you're ready to start producing in your kitchen. Before you preheat your oven or grab a bigger saucepan, let's look at purchasing your ingredients for the best price.

Step 4: Purchase your ingredients

Don't buy all of your ingredients at the grocery store

When you make a small batch of cookies, it's fine to go to the store and pick up what you need. But, when you're scaling up your production makes sense to look elsewhere for ingredients. Try shopping at:

- Natural Food Stores
- Online Retailers like BulkFoods.com
- Food Service Distributors
- Costco and BJ's.

Shopping around has its benefits - the most obvious being cost. And every penny counts in food production.

Buy in bulk if you have the storage

If you've got the storage space, you should buy in bulk. Check out Costco and BJ's Wholesale as well as online bulk retailers to get more of your ingredients in 5,10, or 25+ pound amounts. You get quite the savings!

Not all ingredients are created the same

Before you switch vendors for a less expensive alternative, make your product with the new product. Why? Because not all ingredients are the same. Your flour may be finer than normal. Your jalapenos might be hotter. And, lastly going from fresh to frozen ingredients will dramatically alter your finished product. Keep in mind, though, sometimes cost is not a reason to compromise quality.

How to Store Your Ingredients

With ingredients galore now sitting in your home kitchen, you've got to put them somewhere. Run to a commercial kitchen supply store and buy a couple of food containers. It'll keep everything separated from your normal kitchen food (required by many health departments who let you product in your home) and if you buy in bulk, you'll be able to store more.

A note on storage: Keep your ingredients off the ground. Food should not come into contact with the floor. For commercial kitchens, this means ingredients are kept on pallets. For your house, you could use your kitchen cabinets or food-grade containers on wire-shelving.

With your ingredients shopped for, it's time for the fun part: food production.

Step 5: Setup your kitchen for production

Just like a restaurant, your production line needs to be figured out. Why? Because it's going to be a lot cheaper to produce 300 units of product in six hours than 50, right? Your labor cost would be through the roof?

How do you set up your kitchen for optimal production?

Here are my top 5 tips for producing a food product in your home:

1. Do prep the night before

If you'd like production to go swiftly, do your prep the night before. While you may not have a process ideal for nighttime prep, bakery items are perfect for this. When I made energy bars several years ago, we would mix our dry ingredients in Ziploc bags so they'd be ready to go the next morning.

2. Get everything out and on your counter

Seen the Food Network? Yes, I'm sure you have. Have you noticed how they have everything on the counter in front of them? Or, how 30-minute meals actually get done in thirty minutes? That's because everything is ready to go and in reach. They don't have to walk more than five feet to get something. You can do that, too - especially when your kitchen is on the small side.

3. Have someone watch your process (this is where your family comes in handy) Why would someone watch your process? Because every new set of eyes notices something you haven't. There's an opportunity to make your production more efficient. By having people look at our energy bar process, we went from producing 500 units in 12 hours to producing 500 bars in just over 9 hours, significantly decreasing our labor cost.

4. Invent kitchen gadgets to make your life easier

How did we speed up production? Man-made kitchen tools. We built our own frame to cut the energy bars and an angled piece of food-grade plastic to drop energy bars into their bags (by the way, fighting a plastic bag opening is just plain annoying).

 FOODTRUCKEMPIRE

5. Constantly strive for a more efficient production

This makes sense, doesn't it? Efficient productions do a couple things for you: lower your labor costs (which means your overall cost goes down, too) and spend less time making your product (which means you spend more time selling it). And who doesn't like more money in their pocket?

Ready to produce now? You just want to fire up your oven, right? Not so fast. Here are a couple issues that may arise when you start producing for public consumption from your home kitchen:

1. More on state and federal health regulations

This is the biggy - and the one you have to watch out for. You may not be able to produce your product in your house (even if it's legal to produce). For example, in Vermont, if you gross over $10,000 in sales as a food processor (like mustard, jam and jelly), you are regulated by the state. If you're under, it's free reign. But, that doesn't mean you're out of the woods. There's still labeling requirements, nutrition

facts (if applicable) allergen concerns, etc. Make sure you do your research before setting up shop. Call your health department and they'd be more than willing to help out.

2. Storage Space - it's not just your kitchen

Your new business will take over your entire house. The dining room will be filled with boxes (not your fine china), the kitchen will be obviously littered with extra equipment and 50# bags of ingredients, and your bedroom will become your office where you store piles of paper. It's bound to happen, but it's my advice to let it happen. Renting space is overhead you simply don't need while you're launching your product.

3. Pets

While it's great to have your pet as a mascot for your company, Fido shouldn't be running around in your kitchen anytime you're producing. In fact, some states require you don't have any pets in your house. In Vermont, you can have pets, but they should be put outside while you're producing. We sent our poor pooch to the basement while we made energy bars. It's for your customer's safety. Who would want pet hair in their brownie? Certainly not me!

4. Strain on work/life balance

Trying to find time to make dinner while also making 1,000 energy bars is not exactly the easiest thing to do. That's the situation I often found myself in. My parents and I would be baking through the evening and basically forget to have dinner. Also, conversations tend to revolve around the business, family asks tons of questions about your fledgling food company. Lastly,

you might not be able to hang out with friends on Saturday night because your catering order is due for the next morning. Be prepared for one heck of a shift in your work/life balance.

5. Liability insurance - yep, you need it!

You are producing a food product - something people are going to eat. This means you need product liability insurance. But don't worry! Many policies are around $500 a year and have $1mil in general liability coverage. Call up your local insurance agent (instead of an online broker). You'll be glad you did when you need something done quickly and professionally.

How to know if you're ready for large food production runs

Have you been producing in your home for quite some time? Are you ready to make the leap to a larger commercial kitchen? If so, I've got some nuggets of knowledge for you.

Making the transition from one kitchen to another is almost always a challenge. Just think about moving homes. You have to get reacquainted with the space, find a new place for everything, and figure out what changes you want to make (if you can make any at all).

It's similar to moving your food production.

When you realize you need to make the leap to a larger space, you should be excited, nervous, anxious, and well, jumping with joy! It's a big deal to be the proud owner of a growing food business. Congratulations!

With any growing food business comes growing pains. And sometimes it's hard to address them all so I put together a quick list to make sure you're ready to make the leap to full-scale food producer.

1. Larger cash investment

It's no surprise that moving into a bigger kitchen requires money. How much is the better question. You're probably talking anywhere from $5,000 up to $250,000 for a full fit-up. Be prepared for the cash sinkhole you're about to fall into. Make sure there's enough to not only make the transition, but sustain it, too.

2. Ingredient & inventory management

You'll go from buying 5 pounds of sugar at the grocery store to 50# bags from a food distributor. This takes time, money, and management. You don't want to buy 300# of sugar when you don't need it, right? Tying your money up in ingredients is a risky way to try and remain profitable.

3. Greater pressure to meet revenue goals

A big move means you've got more operating expenses than you know how to handle. When you were producing in your house, you had much less to worry about. Make sure you know how many units you need to sell each month to cover your increased costs. And, what you're going to do to get your revenue back up to where it should be should it take a dive during a busy season.

4. Convince friends and family

This one is always tough. When you know in your heart you want a bigger kitchen, it can be tough to pull the rest of your family on board. While they probably believe in you, they are taking a lot of risk, too. Everyone has skin in the game. Get your friends and family on-board early so they can help you – not hold you back.

5. New health codes & inspections to pass

New building. New health codes. Before you step foot into your new space or sign a lease, give your local health department a call. They'll make sure the building is up to code and you're able to produce your products. And remember, health inspectors have surprise inspections. This means you can't "let that slide" anymore. Keep your facility clean as a whistle.

Think you've got what it takes to make the move to a bigger facility? Great! Keep pushing forward and growing your food business. Let me know if you have any questions!

The quick guide on product liability insurance

There are a lot of reasons companies need insurance. They've got to protect their logo or company name, make sure they're computers are covered, and don't forget workman's compensation.

But, for food producers, you've got to protect something way more important than logos and computers.

You need to protect your customers. Yep - the people who enjoy your products every day. This is why product liability insurance is so important. I recommend getting it before approaching retailers to carry your product.

Why you need insurance:

1. Bad ingredients

If you've got recalled ingredients or spoiled ingredients that were used in production, your customers may be calling you complaining of their upset stomachs. Not good. **2. Allergen statements**

Forget to put an allergen statement on your label? Peanuts, soy, wheat, etc. - it's important to communicate allergens to customers (and in some cases, you're legally required). Get your allergen statement done before you send your labels to the printer.

What kind of insurance do you need (and how much):

Product liability insurance ($1 million):

This insurance does exactly what it describes - protects you from people who have a bad experience with your product. That could be food poisoning or even a shard of glass or metal in your product.

General aggregate insurance ($2 million):

General aggregate insurance is for everything that doesn't pertain to a specific case. This could be property loss, advertising damage, or bodily injury (hopefully that doesn't happen!).

Office insurance (optional):

If you don't run your food business out of your house, you likely have an office. Your office has assets like laptops, office furniture, etc. What if your office gets burned down or flooded? Insurance would protect your tech which means you'd be able to keep your operations going even when you're down and out.

How much does it cost?

Product liability insurance shouldn't cost you more than $300 - $700 annually. This depends on your sales volume. If you're starting out, it's going to take some time to reach the revenue limit that increases your premium.

Besides a revenue increase, you may need more coverage. Here's a couple of reasons:

1. Large distributors

Distributors handle thousands of products. They get your products to retailers and want to focus on that - not your affected product.

2. Big co-packers

Co-packers make your product for you. They don't want to be responsible for your product recall or have any of the liability. After all, they've got their own to worry about.

3. Popular retailers

Large retailers may require a higher amount of product liability insurance. There's more risk if more people are buying your product.

4. Fairs & festivals (where certificates of liability are needed)

When you're sampling food products at an event, the last thing the organizer wants is to be held responsible if a festival goer complains about your food product.

This means you'll need to purchase certificates of liability insurance holding the event as additionally insured. For me, these have cost $25/event, but your agent may charge more.

How to find your insurance provider:

Get national quotes (but buy locally).

One of the best places to find quotes for product liability insurance is national insurance providers like AIG and eInsurance.com - and they might be cheaper than working with a local agent. However, you'll have a much more pleasant experience with a local insurance agency.

Why work with a local insurance agent

I've only purchased insurance from a local insurance agent (who may work for a larger firm) for several reasons:

You get almost instant support

When you work with a large internet-based agency, you probably call a call center to get support. Just navigating through the phone tree is a pain. With local providers, you get a real person on the phone. And you can't replace a real person with a robot, right?

 FOODTRUCKEMPIRE

Work gets done faster

Need a certificate of insurance for your farmer's market or event? Or how about advice on moving to a new plan? Getting work done from your local agent is dramatically faster than a large firm - often less than 24 hours. With a big company, you're lucky if it takes two days.

Partner with a local firm. You won't regret it. They've got the support (and sometimes better quotes), plus, you're supporting a local business.

But some of you may be questioning whether product liability insurance is needed when you're just starting out. I think you know the answer.

Do you really need insurance?

Yes! Product liability insurance is necessary. If you're sued over a bad product, your company might have to shut its doors. There's no one there to back you or your company up.

It's a start-up cost. You need to sell enough of your product to cover the expenses of running a business. And one of those expenses is liability insurance.

Believe me, you'll be glad you have it when you actually need it.

Final thoughts on producing in your house

If you can do it, absolutely produce in your house. Yes, it may mean making your product into the wee hours of the morning, you'll be saving a ton of money. Plus, when you start your company, you won't be 100% sure about whether you're going to continue this past a couple of years.

Home production is the best way to jumpstart your company. You don't have to produce a lot of product, and you'll be comfortable in your own kitchen - rather than an overwhelming commercial kitchen, which we'll talk about next.

10 Tips for solo food entrepreneurs

Are you the sole owner of your food business? Do you do everything from production to marketing, sales to distribution? If so, then this post is for you.

Running a food business all by yourself is tough. Not only do you do everything, you have to keep the company moving forward. You have to find people to help you - even if it means lots of donated product.

Help is out there for you. Including this list of tips below.

I wrote this list because I've been a solo food entrepreneur for some time Yes, my parents help me run the business, attend events, and calm me down when my head explodes at the end of the day, but I'm still the one who runs Green Mountain Mustard. I have no other full-time employees (and my time isn't full-time either).

And with that, I'd like to share a few tips I've learned along the way to make it easier for you, the solo food business founder. And hey, even if you have a team of 10, these tips should be useful to you, too.

Here we go!

1. Schedule out your day in Google Calendar

I started doing this about two months ago. And it's awesome. I have a couple different projects going on right now - everything is color-coded and blocked out each day. I can see where I'm spending my time and what's going on throughout the week. It helps me mentally prepare for each project.

For you, you could break your day into sales, marketing, social media, new store follow-up, show searching, production, etc.

2. Pick up the phone - don't rely on email

An email is easy to fire-off. But, a phone call? You'll get much more done if you talk to someone directly. Thinking about emailing tons of stores in your area? Just pick up the phone, get the buyer's contact information, and hang up - 10 calls in 30 minutes. Then, pack up the samples and you're good to go.

Try not to go the way of the future. Rely on old-school contact methods to push your business forward.

3. Prepare sample kits ahead of time

As a solo founder, you need to find ways to cut down on time. One way is by assembling sample kits ahead of time so they're ready to go when you need them.

Speaking of samples, do you have a system for sending samples to new retailers, press, and online ecommerce stores? You should! Sending out samples takes up a lot of your time.

Want to do it faster? Keep samples on a table with point-of-sale materials nicely packaged. Grab some bubble wrap and a shipping label and head to the post office.

4. Print postage online

Oh, the post office. Part of me is still surprised it's around. But, it does its job. Want a quick post-office hack? Print all of your shipping labels online. Here's three reasons why:

- It's cheaper - Printing online with USPS saves me over $1 a package - every time.
- It's easier - Have you tried filling out a UPS shipping label by hand? It's painful.
- It saves time - Run into the carrier, drop your package off. No waiting in line. Seriously, Go create accounts right now - it's free.

5. Reach out to friends and family

They're always willing to help you out. Whether it's labeling jars, connecting you with store owners, or helping you at fairs & festivals for food producers, family and friends are a food producer's best friend (quite literally).

And the best part? They'll probably work for free product instead of cash. Get in touch with people you know to help you out. And when they need help, you'll be right there waiting. That's what friends are for!

6. Join your state's specialty food association

Look for your state's specialty food association. The annual dues are low and it's a great chance to interact with other people just like you!

I just signed up for the Vermont Specialty Food Association after taking a year off. Now, we're members and excited to begin a partnership with the association. I joined because it's the largest network of small food producers in the state. Basically, a large group of people who know what you're going through.

If your state doesn't have a specialty food association, contact a few other food producers and get together every month to trade notes, stories, and experiences. You'll learn a ton and it'll be a great group to bounce new ideas off of.

7. Outsource what you're not good at

You've seen it before on other small business blogs, I'm sure. Focus on what you're good at - outsource the rest. For example, not so keen on keeping the books, get a bookkeeper. Shy around buyers? Get someone to help with new store sales (although, you should get better).

The more outsourcing your company does, the more time it leaves you to do what you love. Sure, you may have a higher overhead than most companies, but you won't be dealing with the pesky tasks of running a business.

 FOODTRUCKEMPIRE

8. Take a break

What? I thought I was supposed to be getting more done from this list - not less? Yep, you are. But that involves taking breaks, too. Go out to lunch with a friend, head out to the movies, knit a scarf - whatever it is, take a break so your mind can transport you to another space. For me, it's the gym. I make sure to get time there almost every day. It helps to clear my mind and execute better throughout the day.

9. Build it - don't buy it

While this isn't exactly a productivity tip, this is a creativity tip. When you're looking at solutions to solve a problem on your endless list, see if you can make a solution yourself. Through a little ingenuity and some skill, we've built our display, insulated coolers, three banner stands, and more. What I want didn't exist, so I built it.

What can you build? Sketch something out and head to the hardware store. You'll take a break (see #8) and it'll be less expensive!

10. Get a routine down - morning, noon, and night

When I worked full-time, I only had a couple hours each night to work on Green Mountain Mustard (many weekends were taken up by farmer's markets). That meant I needed a routine for when I got home. What do I do? I pick 3 or 4 things I want completed after dinner. And I had a stopping point of 9:30pm when I went to bed.

What's your routine look like? Do you have one? Even if you just have a couple hours each night or the entire day to work on your food business, get into a routine. It helps put constraints on available time and get more done faster.

What to know before you scale your recipes

When you're making two jars of jam on top of your stove, it's simple to understand your recipe. There's sugar, berries, and pectin. You don't even have to weigh anything out.

When you add habanero peppers at a 1:1 ratio, you may get more heat than you bargained for.

But, what happens when two jars become two hundred jars?

A lot. Many food products take a completely different shape when they're scaled up. You might need more sugar to decrease the acidity of your products. You might need more blueberries to get the same intense flavor you had with two jars.

FOODTRUCKEMPIRE

Scaling your recipe isn't as easy as multiplying.

For my own company, I've lucked out that my ingredients do scale with a 1:1 relationship, but some companies aren't so lucky. Here are a couple of products you might want to watch out for when you start to scale your recipe:

1. Produce

Using the same ratio of habanero peppers in your salsa is going to dramatically affect the heat in your products. If you keep a 1:1 ratio, you're going to start breathing fire out of your mouth. Make sure to scale down your pepper ratio 10% or so. The same goes for any produce.

2. Spices

Not all spices are created equally. Some sources are stronger than the others. For example, cinnamon, nutmeg, garlic powder, and black pepper all have varying degrees of strength depending on the amount you use and the brand. Adding too much of one spice could make it over-powering, so start with small batches before you fill the whole oven with over-cinnamoned (like that word?) granola.

3. Frozen/fresh ingredients

This one may seem obvious, but if you're switching from a fresh product to frozen because of better pricing or ease-of-use in larger productions, do a test-run first. Many frozen products increase the water content of your product. This means what used to be a thick & creamy paste is now watery and run-down. If you're using fresh ingredients, you should continue – even if fresh ingredients are more expensive.

Bottom line? Ingredients are temperamental. And you won't know it until you make bigger batches. Your goal is to get the same flavor profile with 200 jars you got with two. It takes a ton of trial and error, but it's worth it. Going into production assuming a 1:1 ratio means lots of money down the drain.

Producing your products on a much larger scale is not easy.

Watch how ingredients scale. Taste-test with family and friends to see which variation comes out on top – and make sure your product is profitable with the new process.

5 Tips to go from Ball jar to glass jar

Going from ball jars to retail glass packaging is a big step for any food business. Here are five tips to help you through it!

 FOODTRUCKEMPIRE

Packaging food products comes with many important decisions. But, when you're just starting out making your mustard, jams, jellies, or pickles, finding packaging that's inexpensive, does the job, and looks nice is tough.

And that's where Ball jars come in.

Ball jars are great for that "farmer's market look", they're inexpensive, and you can buy what you need to the grocery store, hardware store, or even local miscellaneous mart.

However, there are several problems with Ball jars

- Your labels don't stick well
- The jar closure is in two pieces (customer nightmare)
- Expensive when you need large quantities

Sure, for the market when you're making a couple cases of product, they work great. But, what about when your products are ready for retail store shelves?

Making a great first impression requires more than a Ball jar.

I met a jam maker last weekend who just landed her first local retailer. And she's working to make her products visually appealing and store-worthy. One of those strategies is to ditch her canning jar in favor of a sleek 8oz jar – perfect for retail shelves.

She had a couple of questions, so I thought I'd write a few tips to make the transition smooth – for her, and you:

1. Shop around

Making the move from canning jar to glass jar is a big financial move. So, it's best to shop around until you find the best price. You should look at at least three suppliers before you make your decision. Call them up, make sure they service small accounts (some large suppliers brush you off) and that you'll be able to get what you need when you need it. Customer service and support are equally important to the cost of the jar.

2. Participate in a group-buy

Ordering from a large glass supplier makes sense if you need 50+ cases of glass, but to get a better deal, join other food producers in the area and get a few pallets of glass. This dramatically cuts down on shipping costs and ultimately lowers your per unit cost, too. Win-win!

 FOODTRUCKEMPIRE

3. Get a sample pack

When I selected my glass jars for Green Mountain Mustard, this was the best tip I received – straight from the jar salesman himself. Get a sample pack, make a small batch of product, and fill each container. Your product's color, texture, and appearance changes depending on the jar. Many producers are often surprised – what they like empty isn't always the jar they like full.

4. Different jar = different label

When you're considering moving to a glass jar, it might be a completely different shape. And that doesn't mean you should keep the same label you've been using for years. Take advantage of the extra surface and get a bigger label. Maybe you'll have enough room to share a recipe or your company story.

5. Can't pick a winner? Ask your customers.

Ultimately, your customers are the ones purchasing your product. If you're stuck between a couple of different sizes and shapes, post pics to your Facebook business page and let customers vote. Not only will their vote be important, but they're going to want to know what to look for in the store when your packaging changes.

There you have it – five tips to not only take your business to the next level, but be smart about it. Your packaging choices are the most crucial to success because if you're not noticed on the shelf no one will buy your product!

Option #2: Producing in a commercial kitchen

There are a couple of reasons you would need to produce in a commercial kitchen: Either you've outgrown your home kitchen or state regulations prevent you from manufacturing products for public consumption.

It's probably the second one for the majority of you.

State regulations are tough to avoid, but the quicker you get to produce in a commercial kitchen, the more likely you'll get a better handle on ingredient cost, have the ability to increase production, and pass inspections for larger retailers like Whole Foods (more on that later).

 FOODTRUCKEMPIRE

How do you decide if a commercial kitchen is right for you?

Commercial kitchens come in all shapes and sizes. From small 500 square feet facilities that you probably would use just for yourself to larger 30,000 square foot kitchens used by large world-wide companies.

It's intimidating, which is why you need to figure out if you're at the point to make the leap from home kitchen to commercial kitchen (or to commercial kitchen to begin with). Here are a couple signs to help:

How to know if you're ready to transition to a bigger kitchen space

Making the transition from one kitchen to another is almost always a challenge. Just think about moving homes. You have to get reacquainted with the space, find a new place for everything, and figure out what changes you want to make (if you can make any at all).

It's similar to moving your food production.

When you realize you need to make the leap to a larger space, you should be excited, nervous, anxious, and well, jumping with joy! It's a big deal to be the proud owner of a growing food business. Congratulations!

With any growing food business comes growing pains. And sometimes it's hard to address them all so I put together a quick list to make sure you're ready to make the leap to full-scale food producer.

1. Larger cash investment

It's no surprise moving into a bigger kitchen requires money. How much is the better question. You're probably talking anywhere from $5,000 up to $250,000 for a full fit- up. Be prepared for the cash sinkhole you're about to fall into. Make sure there's enough to not only make the transition, but sustain it, too.

2. Ingredient & inventory management

You'll go from buying 5 pounds of sugar at the grocery store to 50# bags from a food distributor. This takes time, money, and management. You don't want to buy 300# of sugar when you don't need it, right? Tying your money up in ingredients is a risky way to try and remain profitable.

3. Greater pressure to meet revenue goals

A big move means you've got more operating expenses than you know how to handle. When you were producing in your house, you had much less to worry about. Make sure you know how many units you need to sell each month to cover your increased costs. And, what you're going

to do to get your revenue back up to where it should be should it take a dive during a busy season.

4. Convince friends and family

This one is always tough. When you know in your heart you want a bigger kitchen, it can be tough to pull the rest of your family on board. While they probably believe in you, they are taking a lot of risk, too. Everyone has skin in the game. Get your friends and family on-board early so they can help you - not hold you back.

5. New health codes & inspections to pass

New building. New health codes. Before you step foot into your new space or sign a lease, give your local health department a call. They'll make sure the building is up to code and you're able to produce your products. And remember, health inspectors have surprise inspections. This means you can't "let that slide" anymore. Keep your facility clean as a whistle.

Think you've got what it takes to make the move to a bigger facility? Great! Keep pushing forward and growing your food business.

But before you start scouting for the perfect space, let's dive deeper and look at a few pros and cons of commercial kitchen space:

Pros of commercial kitchens

It's all commercial equipment

You're not going to use home baking sheets from Wal-Mart or tiny stand-mixers. This is big, industrial equipment. Sure, it's more expensive, but it's equipment that withstands excessive, prolonged use. And it's awesome. Choppers are bigger, Kettles are more efficient. And it helps you make more - higher quality - products. Using commercial equipment truly makes a difference.

Opportunity to expand

Commercial kitchens are an incubator for small food businesses to go to the next level. They represent an amazing opportunity to expand and make your jam side- project into a real business that pays for your mortgage and puts food on the table. Pretty cool, huh?

Experienced staff & scientists

When I first toured a couple of commercial kitchens in my area, I met incredibly smart people - from production managers to facilities managers, and even small business advisors. The bottom

line: You get access to all of this experience when you find a commercial kitchen space where other producers are already making products. Speaking of other food producers....

Community of Small Producers

We're all in this together. Small food producers rally around each other, trade products (the best part), and share resources. There's something magical about it. This community will help you through everything - from looking for new equipment, producing more product when you need help - and even letting you in on the good shows to sell your products.

When you step up to commercial kitchens, things start to come together. It feels like you're actually running a business. But, there are a couple of cons you should be aware of.

Cons of commercial kitchens

Not the right equipment

If you call up a commercial kitchen, chances are they won't have exactly what you need. The kitchen may be set up for dry goods, bakery, acidified foods, etc, All of those applications require completely different equipment. And with commercial kitchens in short supply, it's tough to find the perfect kitchen to use (which is why many producers build their own kitchen).

Expensive

Your home kitchen is practically free. So to spend $25-$100/hour to rent a commercial kitchen is one heck of a financial investment when you've been selling a couple of cases of product a week. Financial investment is necessary to make your mark in the food industry. After all, you've got to spend money to make money. And if you're not willing to spend money, be prepared to not grow as fast. Because growth is expensive. And you need money to make sure you stay afloat. Upgrading to a commercial kitchen space is one of the first steps. And it's expensive.

Distance

You can't make a lot of bbq sauce in your pajamas. You have to drive to your commercial kitchen. And that can be pretty far away. I have several food producer friends who drive up to 3 hours to produce their product in a kitchen that meets their needs. The farther away your kitchen, the more you'll spend on gas. That adds to your overhead, which ultimately takes a chunk out of your profits.

Cleanliness

I have seen NASTY kitchen. And I've seen sparkling ones. Oh, and some that simply clean up when the health inspector comes knocking. Go over protocols for cleaning. Make sure

everything is clean - from the walk-in, to the kettles, packaging equipment, and even the employees. Hate to say it, but do they wash their hands?

Allergens

While I can't certify my mustard as gluten free because of our kitchen you may need to have allergens as a requirement for your kitchen space. When I was talking to the founder of 88Acres (crazy good bars free of the top 8 allergens) she mentioned there was one kitchen certified allergen free for the top 8 allergens. While she pursued the kitchen, she ultimately decided to open her own -- something I'll talk about shortly.

Certifications

If you need a certain certification to state a marketing claim for your product, can it be done in the kitchen you're looking at? In 2014, while exhibiting at the Summer Fancy Food Show in New York City, I was approached by nearly a dozen retailers asking about kosher certification. After researching, I found out I was unable to obtain kosher certification because other products made in the kitchen we used were not certified kosher - and we used the same equipment. The same goes for gluten free, nut free, organic, etc -- they all have strict standards your kitchen must adhere to.

Do the pros outweigh the cons for you?

It's a tough decision. And there may be multiple commercial kitchens to tour in your area. Look at all of them, If you find one you like, push forward. If not, there are other alternatives. If so, explore commercial kitchens more.

But, let's get real for a second. (Sorry, I had to channel my inner Dr. Phil)

Commercial kitchens are not your home kitchen. They have equipment you've never seen. It's a whole new world. There will be a learning curve. And you will face challenges.

Commercial production is what you strive for. You want to make it out of your home kitchen. You want to get beyond the mason jars and Avery printer labels. You want to get into retailers and grow your business.

Growing your business means you might actually be able to leave that pesky day job and pursue your dream.

Option #3: Using a co-packer

Co-packing is covered in the Ultimate Guide to Profitable Co-Packing (this is included in Part 3 of the book you're reading right now in this series – Distributing your food product). It's a special

section of this book for a reason. **Co- packing is one of the most complex decisions any food business owner can make.**

When I owned my cookie company and my energy bar company, all production was in my parent's house. Nightmare.

While planning my mustard company, I made the product in my parent's house until I established demand from my test market (I'll talk about that later, too). However, I knew my product was ultimately going to be co-packed. Simply because I didn't have the funds for space and equipment - but other people did.

The legal side of producing a food product

Before we move on now's the perfect time to download your free Food Business Startup Kit companion guide: https://foodtruckempire.com/fbk-join/. This gets you immediate access to our food business canvas, templates, and interviews with proven food entrepreneurs.

Note: I'm not a lawyer. This is not legal advice, I'm letting you know how you can save your company thousands of dollars.

5 Numbers you need to keep track of while producing product

When you manufacture a food product commercially, there are certain numbers you have to keep track of in case you get a lawsuit or have to facilitate a product recall. Not to mention, it's good business practice.

Batch codes

When you make the first batch of your recipe, you have to assign it a batch code. That helps you figure out when you made the product. There are a few ways to start batch coding. Many small producers use the Julian Calendar method, which states the year ("14" for 2014) followed by the day of the year ("002" for January 2nd). That makes your batch code 14002.

You could also make up your own system.

Large manufacturers have a mix of letters and numbers (lord knows what it means) printed on the side of the cap or the seam of the plastic package. You could use batch #1, batch #2, like JoJo's Sriracha does.

 FOODTRUCKEMPIRE

Whatever method you use, the batch code needs to go on your finished product.

You can sticker it on with a pricing gun from ULINE as shown above.

The pricing gun pictured is a two-line gun because you can also use it to put on your product's expiration date.

Expiration or best-by dates

Expiration dates are important because they let your customer know when your product is about to go bad (even though it "technically" might not -- it could just lose flavor). Expiration dates are set using shelf life testing (if you want to pay for it -- I would if your product is perishable and you know the shelf life is short.).

For example, the shelf life on many shelf-stable condiments is 2 years, whereas fresh-baked cookies are maybe a week or two. And spice blends is an astounding 7 years. Whoa.

Your expiration date is also important because it's used to gauge the life of your product on the shelf. It's used by distributors who, typically, reject a product if it doesn't have 75% of it's shelf life remaining when it hits the warehouse.

The batch code and expiration date need to go on your packaging.

You can use a pricing gun, like the one above, or you can pick up a date coder/embosser for your packaging (the more expensive alternative). But, if you're interested, here's a link to one.

Quantity produced

This one is pretty obvious. How many units of your product did you make? That way, you know how many units were affected by a recall - and how many units you have on hand. This is also important when you're calculating the cost of your food product. If you pay employees (or yourself) by the hour, your labor rate per unit fluctuates.

Temperature

Depending on your food product, you'll need to keep track of all your temperature checks in a temperature log. For example our scheduled process requires us to maintain a fill temperature of more than 185 degrees. My co-packer needs to measure this at several points during the manufacturing process. If it's not hot enough, we wait to fill the jars.

pH & water activity

I'm pretty sure you have no intention of killing any of your customers, right? Right. That's why you have to keep track of your pH if you're producing an acidified food product - like sauces, condiments, etc. If you're making baked goods commercially, you may be required to track water activity, too. A food science lab can help you determine what measurements you need to make - and stay below or above.

Although this may sound elementary, you've got to keep track of these numbers. A lot of kitchens use a binder with a new page for each product produced - that's the easiest way - and all you have to do.

While I'm on the topic of legality, there's another kind of legal precaution you should be thinking about -- the protection of your company's assets and intellectual property.

How to legally protect your company's recipes, fun names, and more

What follows is my story of getting contacted by a large corporation about one of our products infringing on a trademark they had. I spent over $4,300 trying to fight it.

 FOODTRUCKEMPIRE

Don't let it happen to you.

Here's the story (then I'll get to how to protect your recipes, company name, etc.):

Back in July, we received a letter from a lawyer who represented a food company (who's going to remain anonymous because my lawyer said so) asking us to stop using the word "Atomic" on our (now) Ragin' Rooster mustard -- it used to be called "Atomic Rooster", (RIP).

My initial reaction? Oh, sh*t.

My second reaction? This is crap. They've got nothing on me.

There are a handful of products using "Atomic" in their product name: bbq sauce, hot sauce, restaurants, and even the classic Atomic fireball candy.

But, my product was the only mustard.

They wanted me to stop using "Atomic" immediately.

I called my lawyer. Well, he wasn't my lawyer at the time (you know, had to sign the engagement letter and stuff). But, he was one of the only guys I knew who would have my back - and my company's interest at heart. Not to mention, he represented one of the best law firms in the state

Our first meeting cost $367.50.

During that meeting, we reviewed the case and concluded Green Mountain Mustard had a case against the anonymous company. Our lawyer drafted up a letter explaining the relative size of our company, it's limited distribution, and the fact their trademark wasn't well protected. Oh, and a list of "not-too-strong" evidence of other companies using the word Atomic. Even though I found smaller companies (including another in Vermont), no national chains or producers were using the term. While evidence, it wasn't strong.

Regardless, I pushed on.

About a week later, I received another letter from the other company's lawyer. He wasn't happy.

The letter stated that we should discontinue use immediately. If we didn't, the company was prepared to take whatever actions necessary to stop us.

Side note: This company is a multi-million dollar business with distribution across North America. And me? Well, I could barely pay the legal fees to handle this. You get the idea.

I called my lawyer again. He proposed three options:

1. Keep fighting and take it to court

Yes, we could have kept on writing letters back and forth - each letter costing me several hundred dollars. And yes, we could have been sued. But, I wasn't willing to risk it.

2. Ignore the letter

This would have probably resulted in going to court anyone, and we would have had to pay to get out of the suit. Yeah - apparently you can't just "put your hands up" for free. I love you, legal system. Love. you.

3. Change the name and be done with this

It was the easiest solution. I had to print new labels anyway. And getting rid of old labels is a secret pastime of mine. I couldn't pay my lawyers another $3,000. And I couldn't afford the chance of going to court just to save a flavor that, while popular, wasn't widely distributed.

I chose the 3rd option. That meant:

- throwing out the 3,000 old labels (a cost of about $240)
- selling off our current inventory (roughly 600 units)
- changing the name
- ordering new labels

Not a big deal. But still a pain. I signed a binding contract with the other company basically agreeing to the above terms. I had to provide a picture of the new product name on the jar, too (oh, and print new business cards and sell sheets...). Part of me wanted to send them all of my old labels. But, I'm better than that. :)

Anyway......now to the useful stuff. The information you can use to protect your company from the same thing I experienced.

How to build legal assets for your food business

Note: I'm not a lawyer. I never intend to be. And this shouldn't be taken as legal advice. That's why I paid my lawyer $245 an hour. This is simply what I learned through the above legal process.

1. Why protect anything at all?

I've owned my mustard company for over 4 years. I never put thought into protecting anything, until my lawyer gave me three good reasons to start protecting what I've created:

- It's defensive - protect yourself against any legal threats (like the one I got above)
- It's offensive - building a legal portfolio is an asset - not a liability - to your company
- Prepare for sale - while I'm not sure this'll ever happen, you can use your legal assets to increase the sale of your business

2. What can you protect?

While I thought I'd protect everything under the sun, it just doesn't make sense financially. I don't have $25,000 laying around. You might, but I'm sure you could think of a million better things to do with the money. But, legal protection should be on the list because there's a lot to protect:

- Your company name
- Your company logo
- Unique product names
- Slogans and taglines
- Brand marks
- Characters
- Unique packaging (limited, but possible)
- Made-up words (those are fun, but I don't have any) ex: apple for electronics.

Now, you obviously don't have to protect everything. I mean, money doesn't grow on trees. That's why there's this next question.

3. What should you protect first?

I was advised to protect my company name first. Seeing as it's plastered all over everything - labels, cards, banners, etc. I'd never want anyone else to use Green Mountain Mustard (rumor has it in the 1980's there used to be another Green Mountain Mustard, but they never protected the name). Next, my legal team would look at protecting each flavor name.

Side note again: I have "cute" names for all of my products - my customers love them - but they're unique to my company. Things like "horseradish mustard" and "black currant vinaigrette" are commonplace and can't be protected.

I was advised not to protect my logo - the visual part. It's not like the apple "apple" or the nike "swoosh". It's 6 lines that form a mountain. Nothing terribly unique to warrant protection from impostors.

4. Do you really need to protect your logo?

Yes - if you have a distinguishable brand-mark, like I mentioned above in question 3. If it's just text and a couple lines - or clip art you found online - don't bother. It's a waste of money. But, if another company's logo looks suspiciously like yours, you may want to think about protection.

 FOODTRUCKEMPIRE

5. How do you go about protecting anything?

The United States Patent & Trademark Office (USPTO) is your friend. There, you're able to search for any trademark, copyright, or protection a company or individual has ever filed for. If you're a data nerd like me, it's pretty cool. So, before you trademark "Jumpin' Jack's Crazy Jalapeno Sauce" someone might already have protected it (Blast!). Search here first before you invest any money.

You can do this yourself. However, to make sure it's done correctly, I'd advise partnering with a trusted law firm that specializes in intellectual property law. The process is rather simple to file copyrights and trademarks - just a couple pages - but there's a reason people go to law school - to do it right.

You'll get a piece of paper in the mail asking for the filing fee (it honestly looks like junk mail) to be paid within a few weeks. Speaking of filing fees.....

6. What does it cost to protect everything?

To file a trademark or copyright will cost you $375/trademark. In addition to the fee, my lawyer charged me $800 to take care of everything. Again, you can do this yourself, and just pay the $375. This only protects you in the United States. Country specific - or even global filing - is much more expensive and only makes sense if you're exporting products to other countries. Or, if you're just an enormous multi- national corporation.

What I protected with Green Mountain Mustard

I chose to protect my company name - not the logo. Just the word mark. That means, no matter how anyone styles Green Mountain Mustard - colors, fonts, size, etc - I can take legal action. While I believe it will never happen, it's nice to start building my legal portfolio.

When I get a little bit more cash into the company, I'll protect my flavor names. At $325 a piece (if I do the work myself), it gets pricey quick. Guess that means I've got to stop making new flavors, huh?

So, that's all the legal advice I'm going to dole out for now. While I'd love to answer your questions, I'd recommended talking to your lawyer first. They're a lot smarter than me :)

Ok, so let's move on from legal. It's time to talk about packaging. You know, something way cooler than legal protection.

How to package your specialty food product

Packaging is arguably the most important decision for any food company. When you see your product on the shelf, you've got to create such beautiful packaging that it entices a customer

(who is walking briskly by) to stop in their tracks, pick up your product, and contemplate (read: maybe not buy) purchasing your product.

That's how important packaging is.

So important, you're better off paying up-front to work with a designer to get it right the first time. I waited 4 years to have my packaging professionally done.

Here's how this section is going to break down. You'll learn:

- How to come up with creative packaging
- How to design your own packaging
- Packaging ideas for four types of products (bakery, frozen, beverage, & grocery)
- How to source your packaging materials
- What to include on your labels (and where to get them printed)
- How to apply your labels (and other machines to speed up packaging time)
- What to do if you already have packaging lined up

Before I get into packaging, I'd like to address those of you who may already have packaging for your products.

Maybe your products have been on the shelf for a couple months, but your packaging isn't perfect. Is it time for a rebrand?

Let's discuss re-branding real quick:

Branding is the essence of your company. It answers who, what, where, and most importantly, the why behind your company. It sets your products apart from others on the shelf, and it creates a reason for being.

It's been four years since I've changed my packaging. Sure, I've screwed up some labels runs (Incorrect net weights got the best of me when I was starting out), but for the most part I haven't changed anything.

But to me, our brand is getting stale. I'm creating new flavors simply to create new labels – to get new art and a new look for Green Mountain Mustard.

So, with that, I thought I'd go through the pros and cons of re-branding a food company. Yep – it's a list for me. But, it's for you too, in case you're going through the same thing. Let's make it through together.

Reasons to rebrand your product:

1. You want a strong shelf presence

There's only so much room on the shelf. The average grocery store stocks over 38,000 items. That's an overload for consumers. They are drawn to attractive products. Products that stick out from the rest. If your business plan includes a lot of retail sales, you may want to step up your company's design game and get a strong shelf presence.

2. It looks too homemade

Homemade used to be all the rage. It was definitely a design trend in 2012, but homemade is well, homemade. Sticking Avery labels on your products with Microsoft fonts is only going to get you so far. To make it retail and big wholesale shows, you may have to look at re-branding — or simply branding for that matter. Work with a local design or use an online logo creator to start the process off on the right foot.

3. Your company's direction has changed

This is spearheading our rebranding movement. We've simply confused consumers. We have funny-named mustards and classic mustards (with two completely different labels). Plus, we're always launching different varieties at events to keep people coming back. This is an opportunity to create a cohesive brand. A brand that is 100% Green Mountain Mustard – and you know which products are ours on the shelf.

Rebranding is a big decision, which goes far beyond these three reasons. It's a fundamental company shift. Your branding is your story. It represents you. Think about what you're doing. With that, let's look at a few reasons you wouldn't dare to re-brand your food business.

Reasons not to rebrand your product:

1. It's expensive

I'm just starting to price out a rebrand using a small design agency. It's looking like I'll get everything I need for around $5,000. But, that's not the only cost associated with a re-brand. There's new labels, banners, sales sheets, website, and photography.

You're probably looking at another couple thousand to complete the re-brand. However, the goal of the re-brand is to make more money from having a strong brand presence. That means you should see a positive return on your branding investment within the year.

2. Customers resonate with your packaging

Do customers LOVE your packaging? Is it easy for them to find your products in the store? If you answered yes to both questions, then don't change your company's brand. Why? Because customers already know what they're looking for when they head to the grocery store. If you dramatically change your visual brand, you risk a decrease in retail sales because your current loyal customers won't recognize your brand.

3. You think it's "time for a change"

Re-branding just because you want to isn't smart. Talk to your customers first. See what they think. Could your brand use an improvement? Is your packaging communicating what you want it to communicate? Branding is a business decision – not just visual. Give it some thought as to why you want to re-brand. If there's no strategic business reason, keep your current branding. If you think it'll improve sales, go for it!

Now that you've decided to take a fresh look at your packaging, let's get into the first steps. Yes, before you even start to Google for a packaging designer.

All Packaging Starts with a Sketch.

Before you open any software, take a piece of printer paper and sketch what you'd like your packaging to look like. It's ok - it can look horrible. It's supposed to. This exercise is to get your thoughts down and iterate on what you're drawing.

Then sleep on it.

Come back the next day and look at what you drew. Does it make sense? Does it represent the brand you're trying to build?

Here are a couple more questions to ask while you're sketching:

Is the focus the product or the company?

When I decided to re-do my brand's packaging in late 2013 (it debuted in Spring 20134), I wanted to downplay my company name. Sounds crazy, right? But, what we had created is a culture of naming. Our customers loved the product names (and well, our mustard is pretty good, too) -- and, surprisingly, they could have cared less if we were from Vermont. So I decided to downplay the whole Vermont thing, and press forward with a new name-focused design.

 FOODTRUCKEMPIRE

What about you?

Do you feel your brand plays a bigger role than the products your brand supports? Is it more important for you to have the product front and center or the company logo. It's been done both ways for years. Ultimately, it's a strategic decision you have to make.

What does my competition look like?

I could browse grocery stores for hours. Southern Season, a high-end grocery store in the southeast is my obsession. I've been known to spend 2 hours there. It's crazy. But, I'm looking at how other companies have chosen to package their products. Obviously, some packaging is incredibly expensive. But, think about this:

Your products are going to be next to your competitors.

How is your packaging going to stick out? Is it going to be brighter, cleaner, more impactful, bigger, taller - will there be a hang tag, a white cap? How is your packaging going to be distinguishable?

Where will this packaging be in the store?

Grocery stores are packed with products - some on shelves, in freezers, on clip- strips, racks, encaps, buckers, tables, bins -- you name it. Where is your product going to be? My mustard is almost always going to be on a shelf, next to other products that are brown and yellow in color. That led me to create bright, strong packaging never seen in the condiment aisle before.

Looking at other packaging and your product's placement in the grocery store influences the design of your product's packaging. Next up, we'll look at a couple of ways to package different kinds of food products.

How to package your food product

Condiments, Sauces, Jams, and More

You've got a lot of options with sauce-based items. Here are a couple:

- Glass jars/bottles
- Plastic jars/bottles
- Pouches
- Foodservice packaging

The most common packaging style is glass jars because you're selling a high-end specialty food product. Your packaging should look premium.

Now, let's get into a little science.

Most anything liquid can go in a glass bottle or jar - especially if it's hot-filled above 185 degrees. If your sauce is filled into a plastic container, the plastic melts (trust me, I know all too well).

If you're cold-filling (under 165 degrees) your food product, packaging in plastic is, for the most part, a safe bet. I'd still recommend a good seal, though -- like the ones you find on a jar of peanut butter or a shrink-top.

The best way to find the glass or plastic you're looking for is to browse online catalogs and request a couple samples so you can see and feel the container in your hand.

- Andler Packaging (I have used them)
- Birch Bottle
- Richard's Packaging (I currently use them)
- Fillmore Container
- Berry Plastics
- Berlin Packaging
- SKS Bottle & Packaging (great pictures)
- Bottles, etc.
- West Coast Bottles

Why the pouch could be the next best thing in sauce packaging.

There are a lot of benefits to packaging in containers that aren't glass -- just to name a few:

- The package is lighter
- It won't break in transit
- Opportunity for larger graphics & better messaging
- Differentiate your product from the competition

There are drawbacks as well:

- Customer acceptance (what is this pouch thing?)
- High minimum order because almost all pouches are custom-designed.
- Packaging design can be costly
- More shelf-space is needed
- May be perceived as "cheaper"
- Typically only for cold-fill products

When I looked into getting our mustard packaged in a pouch from a Canadian company, the only thing attractive was the price. **Fully-printed, it was 9 cents a unit.** But, I had to order 10,000 of them. And our product wasn't exactly "free- flowing" so it'd be tough to get out of the pouch (customer's would lose mustard that stuck to the walls).

I didn't pull the trigger on the pouch packaging - we still use glass jars. However, the pouch is already revolutionizing the packaging industry. Just look at Campbell's slow cooker sauces. While they do have significant brand presence in the grocery store, the packaging looks amazing on the shelf. You could do this for your product, too, but it will take an upfront investment. **Be sure you have a large distribution before you head down this road.** The last thing you want is a garage full of 50,000 bags and a demand of 1,000 bags a month. You might as well kiss your cash flow goodbye.

Here are a few pouch suppliers to explore

- Flexpack
- Sorbent Systems
- Coveris
- Ampac (great solution for small companies)

It takes a call to a supplier to determine what you need. As you call more suppliers, you'll start to learn the lingo and find what you're looking for.

Pro tip: Work with companies willing to answer your beginner questions. They shouldn't Ignore you. They should be happy to answer your questions - even if your order is a couple hundred bucks or over $100k. Good vendors give amazing service.

And a little note about packaging for foodservice....

While many of you are going to be focusing on retail distribution, there is something to be said for foodservice distribution. While the industry is price-competitive, it can be part of your business model. I'll talk about food service distribution later in the book - for now, packaging.

There are several options for food service packaging:

Larger glass/plastic containers

In 2010, when we just started producing, I thought it would be awesome to make gallon-size batches of our mustard. The problem? We used glass gallons. Not only did they cost close to $4.00 a piece, but they, well, broke. And I couldn't sell them to save my life (more on that later, too). We have since packed some mustard into 32 oz glass jars, but as you probably know, chefs dislike glass containers on the line because they break. And no one wants glass in their

food. These containers, if you choose to use them, can be purchased from the suppliers a couple pages back.

Big pouches

These pouches are just like big pouches some of your ingredients come in -- they're just sealed on both ends. Some, like the ones manufactured by Cryovac have specially designed holes to hook up to those fancy condiment pumps you see at restaurants. And you guessed it -- they're super expensive. Pretty much only for big companies. If you package in pouches, make sure you have a heat sealer to seal the open end.

Single-Serve Portions

Portion cups or pouches are all the rage in fast food restaurants, stadiums, schools, and airlines. But, they also have to be right for your business. Later on, you'll find out why I turned a deal down with a huge airline.

My story aside, single-serve packs are one of the best ways to get your product in-front of thousands of people quickly. The downside is it's hard to get those purchases to convert to retail sales. That's why many major brands have a strong-hold in the market. Fear not, there's a list of suppliers right here if you'd like to jump into the game.

- HS Crocker
- WinPak
- Cuppac (co-packer for portion cups)

Once you've got your packaging selected, let's look at how to fill your containers so that the weight is spot-on every time.

How to fill your sauce into your container - the easy way!

You could hand-fill - FREE

When you're making product on your stove-top, hand-filling makes sense because you're not producing too many units. But, it's simply not efficient. Plus, you'd have to weigh every jar to make sure you have the correct net weight - that's crazy, right? There are better ways to fill your products.

The Handy Filler - $399

While I haven't personally tried this product, it looks like it'll work for thin products (those you can suck through a straw -- not paste products). It's a step up to filling by hand, though.

Single-head Piston Filler - $1,500 (used) - $5,000 (new)

This is what I currently use at Green Mountain Mustard - a single head paste filler (because our product is thick). The benefits: save countless hours, your product is presented nicely in the jar, and there isn't too much maintenance. Here are a couple suppliers (with videos): Gowe, Cleveland Equipment, and TurboFil. There are plenty. These are to kickstart your research.

Multi-head Piston Filler - $10,000 (used) - $25,000+ (new)

Just in case you want to ramp up production on more, you'd be looking at a multi- head piston filler, which is best used on an automated or semi-automated manufacturing line. Those same companies above have multi-head fillers as well.

Let's switch gears and talk about brownies, cookies, and other baked goods. Packaging in this industry is a lot more important because we're talking about extending shelf life.

Packaging your baked goods for maximum shelf life

In 2006, when I was a senior in high school, I started Eddie's Energy Bars (named after my Dad, Ed, and no longer operating). I wanted to see how business worked. While I made a little bit of money, it was nothing crazy. And I learned a ton. Especially about packaging baked goods.

These are your options:

- Bags (there's a lot more science behind your bag than you think)
- Stand-up pouches (they can custom print, too)
- Pastry boxes
- Plastic snap-containers
- Mason jars and other glass packaging (see resources above) First, we'll talk about bags. There are three different kinds you can use: **Polypropylene Bags (PP) $**

These are also known as "cello" bags. They have a crinkly feeling and are crystal clear. They tend to have a better barrier than the PE bags below. And they are a heck of a lot easier to open (your customers will thank you)

Polyethylene Bags (PE) $

PE bags feel thicker. And they're not 100% clear. There is a thin film on the inside. But, the thin film creates a slightly better barrier. These bags, too, come in different thicknesses from 1mil - 5mil. The thicker the bag, the stronger.

Biodegradable Bags $$

While I never used these bags, you can get bags that protect the environment. My friends at Squirrel Stash Nuts use them. Funny thing, though. They have a shelf life of 9 months. Then, the barrier starts degrading. Eventually, your bag no longer exists.

Here are a couple places to browse biodegradable packaging:

- Nashville Wraps
- Marlo Packaging
- Bags & Bows

And an endless list of polybag suppliers...(these are my go-to vendors, though):

- ULINE
- PaperMart
- Bags & Bows
- Associated Bag

If you're interested in printed bags, checkout Interplas.

Now, if you'd like to get a simple plastic bag to store your product in, but then put it in a box -- like crackers, cookies, or mixes, you'd want to get a printed paperboard box. Here are a couple sources for those:

- The Box Co-op
- WS Packaging
- Cactus Containers

How to pick the right sealer for your bag

If you're just beginning, look for a startup sealer on Amazon.com.

If you've made it to the big leagues, congratulations. You've moved past the little table top sealers and are on to bigger and better things. That means you need a flow-wrapper. Flow-wrappers take continuous rolls of film (printed or not) and roll them over your product. Then it gets sealed on both ends.

Depending on your product, you could look into a form, fill, and seal machine, which dispenses your product, by weight into a preform bag, cuts the film and seals it. Both of these machines are well over $200,000. Save your pennies!

Still battling a short shelf-life?

With the energy bar company, I had a 2 week shelf life. And you wonder why we're not in business anymore? I had to guarantee the sale of our energy bars to retailers (we peaked with 20). That means if bars molded, I had to replace them with fresh bars and discount the cost of the moldy bars. The result? Ending up with a tiny check almost every week.

How to increase your bakery product's shelf life:

1. It's in the recipe

Look at the ingredients you use. Some may be sabotaging your shelf life. For example, I used yogurt in the energy bars, which basically ate the bar alive from the inside. Baked items made with mainly dry ingredients and maple syrup or honey (a natural preservative) extends shelf life.

2. Adding Ascorbic Acid

Vitamin C is a preservative, too -- even though most consumers have no idea what ascorbic acid is - and they avoid it. It has a bitter taste, though, so it needs sweetness to balance everything out. That's why a lot of energy bars in particular are loaded with sugar.

3. Increase the thickness and seal of your bag

The thicker your windows are in the winter, the warmer your house stays. The same concept works for baked products. Use a thick bag to increase your shelf life a couple of days. Or, make the seal tighter. I'll talk about sealing methods in the next section.

4. Use a Nitrogen flush

There's a reason your bag of chips is like a pillow when you buy it at the gas station - - and then you find out it's half empty. That's because the rest of the bag has been filled with nitrogen gas to extend the shelf life. This process is incredibly expensive.

Shelf life can be the demise of any business. It can hurt your ability to produce product, meet distributor's needs, and ultimately your customer's satisfaction. Consult a food science lab like the ones mentioned in this guide to discover more ways to get your product stabilized on the shelf -- without harmful chemicals and preservatives.

Packaging Your Frozen Food Product

The frozen food aisle is the toughest aisle to get into in the entire grocery store. There isn't a lot of space. And if you're a small producer, you're often forced out by large producers who literally purchase your product from the shelf to put their products in your spot. It's a brutal (and expensive) industry.

But, that shouldn't stop you from finding amazing packaging to line the shelves of the frozen food aisle. Here are your options:

Thicker bag (depending on what you're packaging)

You'll see the bags mostly in the frozen vegetable aisle. They are form, fill, and sealed like I mentioned earlier, using a thick film with a coating on the inside to prevent freezer burn.

A printed box (with a clear bag or tray inside)

This is how many frozen meals are packaged -- in trays, with wrap, and a paperboard box. Surprisingly, these boxes aren't too expensive -- pennies a piece if you order enough of them.

Here are resources for frozen food packaging:

- Bemis
- ModPac
- BoxCoop
- Ampac Frozen Food Bags

Take time to figure out your packaging. When launching a food product, it's one of the most important decisions to make. It's your brand on the shelf. It should look amazing - but not be so expensive you don't make any money (I'll talk pricing in a couple chapters).

Making your first batch of products

You're now armed with everything you need to know to make your first batch of bbq sauce, brownies, or pancake mix (or whatever you're launching). That's exciting, isn't it? You've got ingredients, packaging, and a kitchen space. That is half the battle right there.

What's next?

You've got to put it all together. Mix your ingredients, put them in your jars or boxes, and slap a label on them. It's time to test the market!

Test marketing validates your product with a small market. You want to know three things:

- Do consumers like my product?
- What do they like about - is there value?
- Are they willing to pay for it?

That last question is important. You could make the best salad dressing, but it could cost the customer $20. No one in their right mind is going to purchase $20 salad dressing. As for the

other two, you'll find this out by asking some friends and family members. But, to get a good idea if your local market loves your products, you want to expand your social circle. Here's a couple tips on how to get the best test marketing for your food product.

5 Tips to test market your food product

Have you been playing around in your home kitchen, trying to come up with the next best chocolate chip cookie? Or maybe, you've got the "secret sauce".

Creating a food product is one thing. But, making a product consumers buy over and over again is tough.

That's why test marketing your new food idea is the way to go.

Test marketing gives you an idea of who would buy your product, for how much money, and if they would change anything about it.

Of course, when you're testing something out, a million things could go wrong. You could get a false sense of hope, you could find out that, while delicious, people won't buy your product. Or, the worst – no one's a fan. (Hard to believe with food products, I know, but it's happened to me before).

So how do you get the biggest bang for your buck from your test marketing efforts? It's not easy. You'll likely be test marketing for several months before you pull the trigger. But don't worry! Once you get an idea for what your customers like, you'll be able to tell what products are going to be a success.

For now, let's get your first test marketing under way. Here's a couple tips:

1. Don't let family and friends give you feedback

Family members are supposed to be honest, right? Not exactly. When I was test marketing my energy bars and mustard, family members often sugar-coated their feedback. They weren't upfront with me. Same with friends – they want to be supportive which means they tell you what you want to hear. This ultimately means you don't get the best feedback.

To find people who aren't friends and family, ask co-workers at work, post an ad on Craigslist looking for focus group participants, or give your family a couple test products and tell them to bring it to work. Since they're co-workers don't know you, they'll be honest.

2. Perfect one product

Test marketing a line of 10 products is overwhelming. It creates decision paralysis for your test group. Plus, it can alter the taste of products if you have them taste multiple varieties. By

focusing on one flavor, you're able to perfect that recipe. Then, when you're successful with one, use your test group to expand your product line.

3. Retailers are not your customers

The first place many companies just starting out go for research is their local grocery store. And that's not a good idea. Sure, it's awesome to get the buyer's attention, but **retailers aren't your customer**. The retailer's customers are the ones buying your product. By staying focused on consumers, you'll get the feedback you need to found a fantastic food company.

4. Prepare for criticism

Let's face it – not everyone is going to LOVE your food product. In fact, just a few weeks ago, I was told one of my test mustard flavors "sucked". I kid you not. While 8 out of 10 customers are likely to think your product is worth buying, it's the other 20% you should pay attention to. Why don't they like it? What can you do better? Taking this criticism and feedback is important. **It helps you make a product 100% of people enjoy.**

5. Craft a 30-second pitch

"Try this and tell me what you think" is probably one the worst ways to get a customer to try your product. It's bland, boring, and not engaging. Work on a short pitch about your product. What makes it different? Do you have unique ingredients? This pitch is not only useful for consumers, but you'll need it when it comes to selling your product to retailers.

Test marketing is necessary to start a food business and produce a product consumers are going to fall in love with. Just making salsa, brownies, or spice blends because you like to cook isn't a great reason to start your food business. Why?

It reminds me of a quote I heard from one of my marketing professors in college:

"Make what people will buy – not what you want to sell."

That quote is spot on. If customers like chunks in their salsa, make it chunky. If customers only want to buy your triple chocolate fudge sauce, then discontinue the other flavors. Focus on what your customers are telling you, respond in a timely manner, and watch your food business take off.

Combine your test marketing with your gut instinct

Believe it or not, your customers aren't always right, especially in the beginning. If you want to launch with a sweet product and a hot product, go for it. If you want to package in glass instead of plastic, no one is stopping you. Sometimes your gut is right. Build the company you want to build with products your customers want to buy. There is a happy medium. You just have to find it.

After you've done your test marketing, it's time to figure out what products you're going to bring to market. This could be a farmer's market, holiday craft fair, or your local natural foods store. Regardless of who you're pitching your product to, **you've got to tackle your finances.**

I know, numbers and accounting probably aren't your strong suit. It's an area where many food producers struggle. That's why this next section is going to walk you step-by-step through the process of discovering how much you should sell your product for.

How to price your food product and still make money

This is the blog post you need to calculate your food product cost and make sure you're making money, too. You know, to stay in business. Super important. I'll walk you through what's included in your cost of goods sold, how to calculate it. etc. And then, we'll walk through how to price your product through the distribution channel. Oh, and examples. Because nothing with numbers makes any sense without examples.

Here we go.

What's included in your cost of goods sold?

Simply put: Anything you do or use to produce a finished product goes into your final product cost. Some people include all the overhead of a business in your cogs, but I won't here because many of you are just starting out. Here's a short list of what absolutely needs to be included:

- Your ingredients (plus shipping)
- Your packaging – plus shipping (jars, bags, boxes, labels, string, etc)
- Your labor (even if you produce in your own house – more on that later)

Why include shipping?

It's part of getting that ingredient to your kitchen. Here's an example of how much shipping makes a difference. You order a 50# bag of flour for $50 – $1/pound. But, it costs you $25 to ship the flour. Your $1/pound flour skyrockets to $1.50/pound. That ultimately increases your product cost. That's why manufacturers order enough raw materials to get free shipping or

spread shipping across more items by increasing the order size.

Why include your own labor?

If you're making products in your house, you have to include labor because, if you don't, you'll lose most of your gross margin when you move to a shared-kitchen or co-packer. For example, if it takes you an hour to make 12 jars of jam, and you "charge yourself" $15/hour, you've got $1.25 just in labor cost.

Pro Tip: Keep track of changes in your cost of goods sold (COGS). When your ingredients, packaging, and labor increase (or decrease, if you're lucky). your total product cost changes, too. In some cases, you'll swallow the increase. In other cases, you'll have to increase your prices. And don't be afraid to increase your prices.

Let's look at an example, now. I'll use Michael's Lemon Blueberry Jam as an example:

Michael's Lemon Blueberry Jam – Ingredient cost

(Note: I'm using fictitious numbers)

Ing	#	Price	Grams	/Gram	Amt	Cost
Berries	50	$175.00	22,680	.008	200	1.54
Zest	5	$57.90	2,268	.026	10	0.26
Pectin	5	$35.70	2,268	.015	25	0.39
Sugar	25	$19.50	11,340	.001	350	0.60

The total cost of ingredients is $2.79/recipe. This recipe makes 12 jars of jam. That means your ingredient cost is $0.23/jar. Now, let's look at packaging.

I'm packing my Lemon Blueberry Jam in a glass jar with a silver lid and a label. Let's look at each component.

Glass Jars:

- 2,400 jars
- $1,896.00 + $300 in shipping
- Total cost = $2,196.00 / 2,400 jars

Cost/jar = $0.91

Lids:

- 2,400 lids
- $300 delivered
- Total cost = $300 / 2,400 lids
- Cost/lid = $0.13

Labels:

- 5,000 labels
- $250 printing
- $75 in plates
- Total cost = $325 / 5,000 labels
- Cost/label = $0.07 (rounded)
- TOTAL: $1.11/jar in packaging costs.

So far, our total product cost is $1.34/jar — and we haven't even added labor yet! Pretty crazy, huh? Let's look at labor:

Labor costs: Let's take the example above, but increase your production capacity.

- 250 jars
- Produced in 4 hours
- 1 person at $15/hour
- Total labor: $60
- Labor/unit: $0.24

Total Product Cost: $1.48/jar

Let's review. If you held a jar of Michael's Lemon Blueberry Jam in your hand, it would cost you $1.48. That includes ingredients, packaging, and labor. Now, you've got the fun part — pricing your product through distribution. That means broker (even if you don't have one), distributor, retailer, and finally, the end consumer – the price on the shelf.

How much do you think your $1.48 jar of jam is going to be on the shelf? Let's find out.

The food industry works on margin, not markup. You can read about the difference here. Before you send your jar of jam through distribution, you're going to want a 40- 60% margin.

Here's how to calculate your margin:

Price to distributors = COGS / (1 – margin %)

Here's how your price changes with different margins:

- 40% margin: $2.47
- 50% margin: $2.96
- 60% margin: $3.70

That's a difference of $1.23, depending on which margin you choose. You want a high margin so you have room to fit a broker's free of 5-7% into your cost structure. Plus, you want to have room for promotions when you start using larger distributors.

For simplicity's sake, we'll say you're going to have a 50% margin. That means you'll sell your jam to a distributor for $2.96/jar. Now, let's look at what your distributor would sell your jam to their retail accounts for....

Distributors usually take another 30% margin.

- Price to retailer = $2.96/ (1 – margin %)

- Price to retailer = $2.96/(1-0.3)

- Price to retailer = $2.96/0.7

- Price to retailer = $4.23/jar

  This means a couple things. This is the price a distributor sells your jam for to a retailer. And, more importantly, this is the price you sell your jam to a retailer. Don't give them a special price. Give them the price your distributor would give them. Now, this cost goes up, if the distributor has to factor in shipping. Let's take a look:

- Price to distributor: $2.96

- Shipping 1,000 units costs $200

- Added shipping cost/unit: $0.20

- Total cost to distributor: $3.16

- 30% margin = $4.51 price to retailer

See how that adds $0.28 to your wholesale cost with some simple shipping? Pretty crazy. Now, let's take the non-shipped cost to a retailer to see what price they'll sell your product for.

- Depending on the retailer, they'll take another margin of between 30% (big grocery)
- 50% (high-end gift shop).

Here's how all the margins play out:

Price to retailers: $4.23

30% margin: $6.04 ($5.99 retail) 40% margin: $7.05 ($6.99 retail) 50% margin: $8.46 ($8.49 retail)

See how your jar can retail for anything between $6 and almost $9 depending on where your product is sold. That's pretty wild, isn't it? Your jar of jam that costs you just $1.48 retails for an average of $7.18?

Don't think for one second that that's too expensive. You make a super-premium product. It demands a higher price than everything else on the grocery store shelf. After all, you've got to make enough money to put food over the table, a roof over your head, and clothes on your kids. The more money you can make, the better. (Yes, it is about the money in the food industry).

And the high price tag is what you charge your customers when you do a farmer's market, fair, or event. That's why events are so great – your margins are sky high and it's great marketing – a win-win, if you will. Where else can you make $5.52 per jar in gross profit (that's profit before operating expenses)?

Let's look at how different it would be if you took a 60% margin, your distributor took 30% and high-end retailers took 50%. In that scenario, your jar of jam would retail for a whopping $10.57! Whoa, baby!

A quick note about testing your price.....

Will consumers pay for a $12 jar of jam? Maybe. You'll have to find out. Or, does 4x the jam move when it's $3.99? No one will know until you test your pricing. And if you find consumers will pay less, you might want to see if you can cut your costs down. With that being said, you still need to make money. A higher price point may be the only option for now.

A little tweak goes a long way......

After you've established pricing, you should focus on decreasing costs. That usually means buying more ingredients in bulk, glass by the pallet, or increasing the number of units you can produce in the same amount of time.

Let's look at how much more profit you'll make if you decrease your cost just $0.10/unit.

- Cases sold per month: 400
- Units per case: 12
- Total units per month: 4,800
- Monthly savings: $480
- Yearly savings: $5,760

This example shows how important it is to pinch every penny.

But, it's also important to hold your prices where they are. A decrease in costs doesn't mean a decrease in price. Let's pass the $0.10 decrease in COGS through the distribution channel:

- New product cost: $1.38
- New price to distributor (50%): $2.76
- New price to retailer (30%): $3.94
- New price on the shelf (40%): $6.56

So, the price comes down significantly, but a retailer will likely round up to $6.99 to increase their margin. They may go to $6.59 or $6.79 to make it a more "familiar" price to the consumer, but I wouldn't stretch your luck. (Side note: does pricing blow your mind, too?)

There's so much math! What does this all come down to?

It comes down to this.....how much money do you want to make? Do you want to make $60k a year from your food business? Maybe $100k? Whatever the number, you can use your pricing to figure out how many units you need to sell every week/month/year. Let's see what it would take to make $60k a year – that's a net profit of $5,000/month.

 FOODTRUCKEMPIRE

All through distribution:

- COGS: $1.48

- Price to distributor: $2.96

- Gross Profit Margin: $1.48

- Operating expenses (30%): ($0.44)

- Net profit margin: $1.04

- $5k profit = 4,807 units (401 cases)

All through direct-to-retail sale:

- COGS: $1.48

- Price to distributor: $4.23

- Gross Profit Margin: $2.75

- Operating expenses (30%): ($0.82)

- Net profit margin: $1.93

- $5k profit = 2,591 units (216 cases)

All through direct-to-consumer sale:

- COGS: $1.48

- Price to customer: $7.00

- Gross Profit Margin: $5.52

- Operating expenses (40%*): ($2.21)

- Net profit margin: $3.31

$5k profit = 1,510 units (126 cases)

* Operating margin is higher due to the high cost of direct events

Now, most companies use a blend of all three channels – distribution, retail, and direct – to grow their business. But, you can see how going direct to retail – or to the consumer – is the way to increase profits. This shows you how much product you need to produce and sell every month to sustain a profitable food business.

Pricing is not simple.

It's a complex animal that is constantly evolving. You have to stay on top of it, scrutinize every penny, and make changes where you see fit. That may mean changing your business model, increasing/decreasing your pricing, or cutting down on your operating expenses.

If you learn one thing from this part of the book, it's this:

You are in business to make money.

If you make jam that costs you $2.00 and sell it for $3.00 at a farmer's market, you won't make any money when you sell your product through the distribution channel. If you have dreams of selling your product in stores, all of this pricing has to be taken into account. And if you use broker's, make sure to add in that extra 5-7%.

Business is tough. Pricing your product right helps alleviate some of the risk because now you know you'll be making enough money when you sell your jar of jam to customers.

Why you still need working capital

Working capital is the money you need to keep the lights on -- to keep the business moving forward. For example, in addition to paying yourself a monthly salary, you need to have the cash to pay for packaging, ingredients, labor, rent, etc.

That is working capital. And you need it.

This is just a simple reminder that it isn't all about paying yourself from what's left over at the end of the day. You need to keep the business moving forward. For example, I had times in my company where I made a couple thousand dollars the previous month, but it needed to go right back into the company to pay for more finished product.

 FOODTRUCKEMPIRE

I'll go deeper into financials later in this book to see how everything is related to each other. For now, keep working capital in mind.

Next, we'll switch gears and talk about one of the best ways to validate your product line and make some money doing it. Ladies & gentleman, here we go.

Part 2:

The Ultimate Guide to Building Your Business With Farmers Markets

 FOODTRUCKEMPIRE

The ultimate guide to building your business with farmers markets

Farmer's markets are popping up all over the country. You probably shop at one or two weekly during the summer (and for some, winter) to pick up produce, local meat, cheese, and maybe a jar of your favorite hot sauce.

Have you ever considered selling your product at the farmer's market?

(The answer should have been "Yes, Michael, I have"). You should have no excuses to want to sell your product at the farmer's market. Yes, you have enough time. Yes, your product looks fine for the farmer's market. Yes, you'll get into one somewhere. And yes, you'll make money.

When I first started with farmer's markets in 2007 selling homemade energy bars (remember, many states allow home bakery licenses), my display was ugly. My packaging was clearly homemade, but people purchased. They loved my product, the story, and the fact I was making it happen at just 17 years old.

I used the farmer's market to launch my business. Was it a gangbuster success? No. An average Saturday for me was $150. For 6 hours of work, that was way more money than I was bringing in from my retail job at a party store. It was this mini- success that propelled me to explore how I could make this a bigger business.

- How could I generate more sales?

- How many markets could I attend a week?

- What'll happen if I change my display? Will sales increase?

I've researched these questions over the last 7 years selling at farmer's markets (when this section was written), ultimately coming up with

- The best displays to get consumers interested
- The right pricing model to increase sales
- The correct way to pack everything into the van
- How to get on the market manager's good side :)
- How to hire and train salespeople when I'm unable to attend

.....and lot's more. It's all in this section of the book. Just like the Ultimate Guide to Profitable Co-Packing (included later in this book), **there is a TON of useful information here.** It's perfect

 FOODTRUCKEMPIRE

for you if you're just getting started with farmer's markets or you're a 20-year veteran. Everyone will learn something they can apply to their market next weekend!

Let's get started with the basics.

How to find your first farmer's market

You probably know about every farmer's market within a 50-mile radius of your house.

But, your best resource is going to be other food producers already selling at farmer's markets. They know which ones you'll do well at -- and hopefully they won't convince you to do a market you won't do well at!

If you know a food producer (how could you not these days?), send them a quick email to ask about the markets. They'll not only let you know about the ones they do, but they'll probably connect you with the Market Manager, too.

You can also find fairs & festivals, too.

A little backstory as to why this is important:

I just returned from a festival in southern Vermont this past weekend. I got hosed. A whopping $230 in sales. Which really means I lost about $250 for the weekend after hotel, gas, and food were taken out of the equation.

So, what went wrong?

Simply put, vendors were misinformed. The event organizer expected 20,000 people. The actual attendance? Probably 5,000. And the worst part? They were sampling like crazy and not buying.

I brought 17 cases of product and sold less than 4.

Isn't there a lesson learned for every experience? If you're going to lose money you want to know beforehand so you can save your hard-earned cash.

So what did I learn?

I was simply filling the calendar – not investigating whether this was going to be a good show for us or not. For example, we typically don't do 4th of July parades, events with a small number of vendors, and shows doing the first quarter of the year. But, those are our criteria (see tip #4 below).

For the bigger picture, I wanted to write down a list of five things to do when you're selecting a show – so you end up making some money – not losing it.

How to find the best fairs and festivals:

1. Ask other vendors

This is the best kept secret many food businesses don't talk about – their best shows. While many keep their show schedule a secret, you can often find an entire year's worth of shows on producer's Facebook pages, and company websites.

Or, if you meet them at a networking event or other fair, just ask. We're all a big community willing to share information.

Bonus tip: Avoid simply copying another producer's show schedule. Pick a handful of shows and see if they work for you. Then, add more in as cash becomes available.

2. Ask your customers

You want to go where your customers are, so why not ask them where they shop? What events do they attend? It's likely they've been going for years and would have a good grasp on whether your product would be a good fit or not. Plus, you know you'll have at least one sale!

3. Join festival newsletters

There are several festivals newsletters to make sure you're on-top of your game getting applications in. A few good ones are FestivalNet.com and SunshineArtist.com. With shows listed across the country, there's something for everyone.

4. Develop show criteria

There are thousands of shows to choose from. There are art festivals, music performances, food festivals, and parades (personally, not my favorite). How do you narrow them down? With a list of criteria. How many people attend? How far away is it? How many days is the event? Do I need to hire help? Answering these questions helps you decide what shows are the best fit for your company – which makes the decision process easier.

5. Keep your budget in mind

Remember, it's not just the show fee you're paying. You've got gas, hotel, labor (if you need to hire a team), eating out, parking, etc. That adds up. A show with a $495 booth fee quickly becomes a $1,000 weekend. The more expensive the show, the more product you need to sell.

Often in your first few years of selling, you're trying anything. There will be hits and misses. Finding the right shows takes time.

With these tips, you are now better equipped to make a decision about your next show being a cash cow or a total dud.

Once you find your market, it's time for research.

All markets aren't equal. Here's a list of what to look at when you're identifying a market to apply to:

How many vendors are there?

Number of vendors is a sure sign of economic health for the farmer's market. For example, I've done a farmer's market with 10 vendors. We didn't make a lot of money each weekend. Now, our only market is 92 vendors. It generates over $2 million a summer. Big markets have lots of vendors - at least 25. Of course, there are drawbacks when the market is huge.

Are there vendors with similar products to yours?

I'm a fan of competition because it makes you work harder to make a better product, sell harder, and build a loyal following. But, some markets don't allow for direct competition (mainly the smaller ones). Look around the market. Are other vendors selling honey, cookies, or drinks? That may mean you don't have a great chance of getting in, but nothing ventured, nothing gained, right?

Is the Market Manager present?

Some Market Managers run the market and don't play an active role in growing the market -- more vendors, revenue, and diversity. I look for Market Managers constantly on the move, building relationships with vendors (regardless of seniority), and running the show like it's their full-time job. This provides you with an opportunity to inquire about applying to be a day vendor or seasonal vendor for next year.

Who is walking around?

Demographics! I know you think only marketing majors care about demographics, but you should, too. Farmer's Markets pop up in affluent towns, poor neighborhoods, and large urban parks, all bring a diverse population to the market each week. Use tools like ZipSkinny.com to discover household income, education, children, and more. Generally, you want one of two things -- an affluent area whose residents support the vendors and/or tourist heaven.

 FOODTRUCKEMPIRE

Would your products compliment the market?

Does another vendor sell something your product would go great with? For example, our mustards are perfect for any grilled item. Several times throughout the market, we'll partner up to do some cross-selling. What's this mean for you? If the committee who selects vendors notices your product goes with other vendor's products, you're likely going to get in more easily than someone with competing products.

Are Vendors Friendly?

With 92 vendors at the Burlington Farmer's Market, I don't know everyone, but we're all like family. Everyone is approachable and willing to bend over backwards to help. Talk with a couple vendors, ask some questions, and make a friend. Friendly, happy vendors = a successful farmer's market.

What's the weather like? (Seriously)

You probably think this is a stupid question, but our farmer's market runs 25 weeks out of the year - and it can be cold, windy, & rainy at the beginning and end of the market. If you're in a coastal town, it can be worse. Take your area's weather into account when evaluating which farmer's market to apply to first.

These questions are important to ask because you need to spend your time at markets that make you money. If you've found a couple worth checking out -- I'd limit yourself to 4 a week (it's a lot more tiring than you may think), then it's time to apply.

Let's look at how you can make your application stand out.

How to get your farmer's market application noticed

Applications are available on the farmer's market website -- or you can ask the Market Manager to add you to the list of possible vendors who they send an application to annually (usually via email).

1. Sell something not sold at the market already

If you sell something three vendors already sell, you can probably guarantee you're not going to get in. You may get in as a day vendor (who subs when a permanent vendor can't make it), but there are no guarantees. That means the best way to get noticed is to sell something the market has never seen before.

2. Support local producers

Working with farmers to use their produce in your products is a sure-fire way to get to the top of the consideration pile. Many applications ask who you're working with, so make sure to include a couple local businesses.

3. Send Samples (if requested)

So you make the world's most amazing empanadas? (I'd love to try them). If you're allowed, get samples in front of the selection committee. Find a way for them to sample your food products - after all, a pitch in person is way better than a pitch on paper.

4. Take time to fill out your application.

Tell your story, attach pictures (if requested), and get your application in early. This not only shows your initiative, but you'll have the most important task done. That means more time to focus on growing your sales at your farmer's market debut.

A quick note about being wait-listed....

Our first farmer's market was in Williston, the next town over from us. We didn't do the farmer's market in our own town because there were too many vendors. It was a slow market - maybe $150 - $250 a weekend. Enough to meet the financial needs of a student.

We added a second market -- the Essex Farmer's Market on Friday nights. It was a better location, more lively, and we pulled in $250 - $350 a market (on a good, non- rainy day).

But, I heard of greener (read: more money) pastures...

The Burlington Farmer's Market was where I needed to be. While it was 5 - 6 times more expensive than our current market, it attracted between 5,000 and 8,000 people every weekend. And for Vermont standards, that's PACKED.

Many of these customers were tourists from southern New England....**with money. We applied thinking we were a shoe-in.**

No one was selling mustard, I was young, and had built a small following. **Wrong.** I was on the waitlist for 2 years before I became a substitute vendor.

Our first season, we were at the market sporadically -- maybe four or five markets And it was usually raining. We still did well - $300. In the rain.

Now, we're a full-time summer vendor.

Green Mountain Mustard has now been at the Burlington Farmer's Market three seasons -- two have been full-time. And over the course of 6 months, we'll pull in $13,000 - $15,000 -- averaging $520 a market. Our best market was $816.

My point? The waitlist is not the end of the world.

Keep applying. Maybe you'll get in as a substitute vendor next year. Then, be nice to everyone, create a great impression with customers, and apply again. You're more likely to get in with some experience under your belt -- and the willingness to come when the weather sucks (that means you're dedicated to the market!).

Don't get discouraged.

Keep applying. Look at other markets in the next town over. Sometimes it's better to start small anyway. You'll get a chance to learn how farmer's markets work, talk to your small legion of customers, and prepare yourself for bigger, more lucrative, markets.

What if you get accepted? What's next?

First off, congratulations! Getting in your first farmer's market is an amazing feeling. You get to share your creations with your community.

But, it also comes with a ridiculous amount of planning.

- What will your display look like?

- How will you package your product?

- How much do I sell my product for at markets?

- How much product should I bring?

- How much change should I bring?

- Are you going to have any special deals?

- When do I need to get there?

- What if it's raining?

- Will everything fit in the car?

- Do I need any help?

 FOODTRUCKEMPIRE

- What if I don't sell anything? (Yeah - that would suck, but with the tips coming up, you'll be going to the bank with a smile on your face).

See? TONS of questions arise when you've never done this before. Let's tackle one at a time.

What will your display look like?

Displays are going to make or break your sales. If you have a simple display, you may get passed over. If you have a complex display, customers may get overwhelmed (and it'll take you forever to setup).

I work with three guidelines when I'm designing a display (which I tend to re-design each summer:

1. Do customers know what I'm selling?

It's taken me four years to nail this one down. I always get asked "What is this?" or "Is this hummus?" (no). Make it clear what you're selling. When your product is in jars or bags, it's hard to know at a quick glance what you're selling.

The solution?

Get a couple banners. We have one banner that goes at the back of our tent. It has our logo and a call-to-action to get more mustard on our website. It's simple, clean, and a splash of color.

Now, this is optional, but I have a second banner that's almost the width of our tent that simply says "MUSTARD". It gets hung on the outside of our tent so customers can identify from the other side of the market what we sell.

Where do I get my banners?

I got all of my banners printed at DesignToPrint.com in Utah. You get a quality banner shipped to your house for a lot less than Staples or Vistaprint. Plus, it holds up in all weather scenarios. And get grommets in your banner, They help attach your banner to your tent.

Another idea (which I haven't implemented) is a table-top sign. I wouldn't add another "MUSTARD" sign, but you could add the flavors you have to sample.

Design and print a sign at Costco (it'll cost you less than $1) and frame it up at WalMart (or if you have an IKEA, go there. And lucky you!).

2. Can customers easily access samples and product?

Barriers to sampling are barriers to sales. Having customers ask for samples is tough. They have to go through a decision process...

- What the heck is this?
- Do I like it?
- Do I want to taste it?
- Does the guy behind the table look approachable? (more on that later)
- What flavor do I want to try?
- Do I have to ask for a sample? Oh, I do?

And that's when your customer either runs away or asks you for a sample. That's a lot of internal questions they're asking. To avoid this paralysis, make samples available to passer-bys. If they're intrigued, they'll grab a sample. If not, they simply walk by.

Some food business owners have told me they like to strike up a conversation -- in other words, force people to talk to you. That's why they withhold samples.

I get it. And sometimes it works.

But, when there are a lot of people, such as at a fair or festival, holding your samples hostage is a bad idea. Get your product in as many mouths as possible - and do it quickly. Sure, some health departments prevent you from doing this, but when they don't, SAMPLE!

3. How fast can I set it up? Can it be set up by one person?

Your first farmer's market is likely going to be a complete disaster. You'll forget things, realize it takes much longer to set up your display than you thought, and it'll be a stressful experience. Remember, it's all for the customers, though!

What does all this mean?

Make your setup simple and possible for one person to set up. It's awesome to have a second person help, but keep in mind you're probably going to be alone for a good amount of weekends -- or you might have two markets on the same day. That's a crazy thought for right now, so I'll stick to your first market.

Our first market.....

I was selling energy bars at my first farmer's market. I bought a small green tent -- the Quest brand that falls apart after 2 years of hard use. It worked as our first tent, but I quickly upgraded to a white EZ-Up Tent. Then, a tent from Costco (we have both now).

I bought product in a cooler and quickly realized our chocolate varieties were going to melt in the sun....and they did. Our samples dried out in the sun, too. Disaster. It wasn't pretty.

Fast forward a few years and we have an incredibly optimized display, perfect for a large sedan or a van (that was one of my requirements as my Dad and I were designing the new display. Our basic setup can be brought to life and packed up in under 30 minutes. Efficiency at its best.

Here's every piece of our setup:

- Bin for all miscellaneous items (get a sturdy one)
- 6' folding lifetime table
- Tablecloth
- Trash can
- One-piece sampler (picture)
- 2 wooden boxes (open ends to store bags and business cards)
- A wooden stair (from Home Depot)
- Back Banner (3' x 7') + bungees
- Top Banner (2' x 8') + PVC poles and rope
- 10x10 EZ-Up Tent
- Dolly with plywood to maximize load

Other pieces (optional):

- Wood to level table when we're outside
- Extra 4' table to process orders faster
- Clipboard with email signup
- Chairs (I never sit)

You don't need much. And don't overcomplicate it. You need a setup that's quick, easy, and cheap. Our display does that, but use my display materials as a reference.

You may own a small home bakery or prepared foods business. That should be setup differently. With baked goods, it's all about grabbing attention, varying heights, and clear pricing.

With prepared foods, there are different health department rules you must follow, but think about using pictures to describe the food -- and again, price clearly. **Try to eliminate the "How much is it?" question.** Customers always ask, but less will if your pricing is obvious.

4 Ideas for displays and why they work

So, what's a good booth design look like?

Let's get started. Here's the first display:

1. The Clean Look

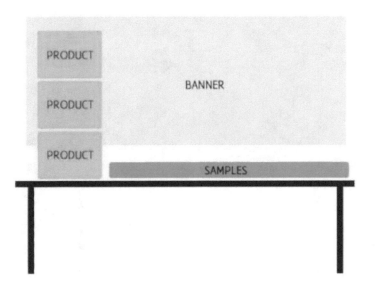

Having been to a handful of farmer's markets and seen over 1,000 booths, certain booth displays work – and others simply don't. And a display is crucial to pulling more customers into your booth to sample your products.

Below, you'll find four displays that work incredibly well. Some of them I've used with Green Mountain Mustard. Others have been suggestions from market vendors.

Why this display works:

This is the display I use for Green Mountain Mustard. It works because the product is stacked high, like grocery store shelves. It creates a shopping experience for customers. Popular products are kept at eye level, shelf-talkers highlight new products, and it's clear how sampling works. A large banner is used to display company name and branding.

2. The Commanding Presence

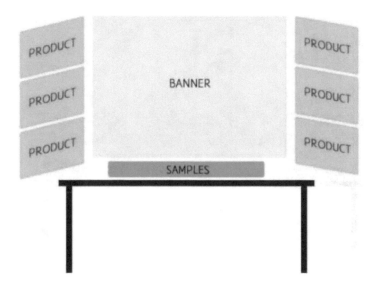

This is the display I use for Green Mountain Mustard. It works because the product is stacked high, like grocery store shelves. It creates a shopping experience for customers. Popular products are kept at eye level, shelf-talkers highlight new products, and it's clear how sampling works. A large banner is used to display company name and branding.

Why this display works:

In this display, you're using two large shelving units that flank a banner in the center.

This creates the visual appeal of a lot of product, and the banner in the center helps to focus your customer's eyes on your company. Samples are placed at a table in the front, and product is grabbed off the shelves as it's ordered

3. Varied Heights

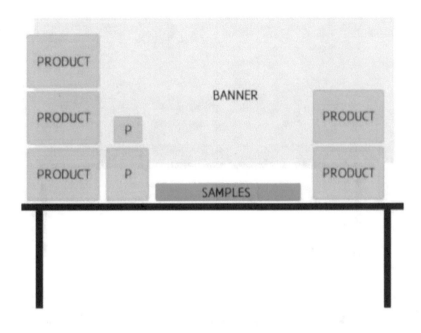

Why does this work?

This works because of the different tiers of product. Large products, like 9 oz jars are kept on the bottom. Smaller products, like 4 oz jars are displayed on top of larger product in a different container (preferably with a small sign to differentiate the products). Using alternative merchandising pieces helps to give this setup its appeal.

4. The Long Shelf

```
                    BANNER



              PRODUCT
              PRODUCT
              SAMPLES
```

This works because of the different tiers of product. Large products, like 9 oz jars are kept on the bottom. Smaller products, like 4 oz jars are displayed on top of larger product in a different container (preferably with a small sign to differentiate the products). Using alternative merchandising pieces helps to give this setup its appeal.

Is there a perfect display?

Best for companies with large product lines (like jams & jellies), this display works because of the wide array of product viewable to your customer. There are clean lines and samples are below each product's row making the customer's experience nice and easy.

No way! Over the past five years, my displays have changed several times a season. It's all an experiment to figure out what works for you and what increases sales.

Hopefully these farmer's market display ideas give you inspiration for how to set up your booth and generate more sales at the farmer's market.

You want one thing from your display: height

That's where my number one tip comes in: height.

Use height to make your booth inviting

If you're a new vendor, creating a display can be tough. You don't quite know how your display is going to look compared to other vendors, and you want to sell as much product as possible, right?

Of the thousands of farmer's market booths I've seen, display height has always made a difference in which booths I walk into. They're store-like – with shelves, tons of product, and they're clean.

Think of your booth as a grocery store – a 10×10 shopping paradise. Walk into a grocery store in your area and you'll notice different heights all over the place – from traditional shelving, to produce displays, and decorated end-caps (the ends of the aisle).

Incorporating height into your display

The best way is with a shelving unit. We've either hand-built ours with scrap wood in the garage or you can pick up metal shelving from stores like Lowe's. It's super easy to put together, throw in your car, and you're off. The shelves are adjustable to fit small 4oz jars or bottles of salad dressing. For a first shot at a great booth, this metal shelf will be just fine. Use the front part of the shelf to advertise pricing and market specials.

Observe your customers

Watch how customers shop your shelves and adjust accordingly. For example, one of our shelves has six facings of product – three of each of our most popular flavors. And we have an entire shelf devoted to limited edition products.

I can guarantee customers stop just because of the height of your display. If you have a smaller table with one level of product, it's hard to tell from the distance what you've got so raise it up!

Three More Tips for a Great Farmer's Market Display

1. Get Signage

2. Brand Your Booth

3. Keep Shelves Stocked

Banners are your best friend. They're often under $100 and easily communicate your company name, location, and what you're selling. Looking for a source? I get mine from Design to Print.

You've got company colors, right? Consistent branding is key for a farmer's market is important because it makes your company recognizable to repeat customers or locals who have seen your brand on store shelves. From coordinating banners, to tablecloths, and fonts, make everything relate back to your brand.

Overflowing buckets and fully-stocked shelves are a sign that you've got what your customers need. In other words "there's plenty more where that came from." It ceases the customer's mind and looks more professional.

4 Ways to hold down your farmer's market tent

How are you going to hold your tent down?

You probably use the EZ-Up 10×10 white tent. It's basically the farmer's market standard to shelter you from wind, rain, and the occasional sleet.

But how do you hold your tent down?

That question was posed to me at the winter farmer's market by my talented jewelry- making friend, Marsha. After all, she didn't want the tent to fly away!

It's tough when you can't set up your tent on grass. Maybe you're on pavement or half on a sidewalk. You don't have the opportunity to simply stake down. This means you've got to do something to keep it from taking off. One windy day and your tent is going for a trip. I've seen it happen five times.

4 solutions to hold down your tent:

1. Gallon jugs filled with stones

This is how we've been holding our tent down for three years – and it's never failed. Save up some old gallon milk or vinegar jugs. Run to Home Depot and pick up a bag of stones (surprisingly inexpensive). Fill the jugs with stones and screw the top on. Suspend with rope from all four corners of your tent and you're good to go. Does it look pretty? Not really, but it gets the job done.

 FOODTRUCKEMPIRE

2. Weighted plates

Have some old plates from you or your husband's lifting days in the garage? Grab a couple of ten pound weights and hang them with rope from your tent. Finally putting those dusty weights to good use.

3. Screwing the tent legs into cement-filled buckets

I'm sure the employees at Home Depot would love you. Buy four small buckets and fill them with cement mix. Drill two holes (to match the bottom of the tent leg) and grab some screws from your work bench. A tent screwed into cement? It's not going anywhere.

4. EZ-Up weighted bags

These are going to hurt your wallet – $54 on Amazon. Plus the cost of sand to fill the pockets. They combine for 40 pounds of weight, so they'll definitely hold your tent down. My opinion? They're hardly worth the money. Get creative with one of the solutions above first.

How to package your products for the farmer's market

You'd think simply bringing your products to the farmer's market means they're going to sell. Not necessarily. You have to think about how you're going to package them. Are your items going to be boxed up in a variety pack, grab-and-go, or sold by the unit.

Customers love single units, bulk discounting (which increases your revenue per customer), and, near the holidays, like variety/gift packs. I've tried to sell mustard in packs before and it didn't work well. Although people may have been buying for their father, cousin, or sister, they didn't need the excess packaging. So, that means you should save the environment, cut the excess packaging, and sell everything by the unit.

Should you have more than one size container?

(For example, we exclusively pack our mustard into 9 oz glass jars).

Once upon a time, I packaged in 4 oz jars, 32 oz jars, and 128 oz gallon jars. Here's why I no longer do any of that:

1. Streamlined production

My product is co-packed which means the more I can streamline production, the better. Adding different sizes into production - small or large - is inefficient. It's more efficient for me to run

multiple kettles of the same (or two) flavors. That way the entire packaging line doesn't have to shut down to make the switch on the filler, packaging, labels, and boxing.

2. Poor demand

I noticed people were asking for a smaller sample pack only during the months of November and December. We could make 4 oz containers, but you can't carry those on the plane. I could go with 2 oz, but who wants a knife-full of mustard? No one. There simply isn't the demand for small containers -- or large for that matter.

3. Higher margins

When we sold different size containers, we competed on price. That hurt our margins. Customers wanted 4oz containers for half the price of a 9oz (which cost roughly the same amount). They wanted gallons for $15. That just wasn't working for us.

It's for these three reasons, **we stick with one size jar**. Everything is simpler -- packaging, sell sheets, pricing, etc.

Speaking of pricing, it's the next question to answer.

How much do I sell my product for at markets?

This one is pretty simple: Sell it for the price it'll be on the shelf at local retailers. There are 3 reasons to do this:

1. You don't undercut your retailers

If customers know they can get your product directly from you for a significant cost savings, they're going to do that. Meanwhile, you'll be wondering why sales haven't picked up at your local retailers. Don't undercut. Remain competitive.

2. You make higher margins (MORE MONEY)

High margins are one of the best reasons to sell at farmer's markets. Match your retailer's price, and you have yourself a fantastic margin. You can earn $4-5 on every unit (sometimes more) you sell. Sell a couple cases and you're making money!

3. You establish price points with customer

The price they pay to you should be the price they pay in the store. That way, when they go to the store to pick up your product mid-week, it's not cheaper or more expensive. Pricing consistently is important. You establish a little more trust and credibility along the way.

 FOODTRUCKEMPIRE

Now, with that being said, we do have a few retailers who sell our mustard for $5.69. I sell it direct for $7/jar, but if you buy 2 jars (which 80% of my customers do) you're down to $6. And I like to round up. I'm not going to sell mustard for $5.69 only to begrudgingly give customers back 31 cents.

A quick note on offering deals:

Some vendors do not like to offer deals. But, the truth is, deals increase your sales. Why do you think department stores always seem to have half the store on sale? It's because it gets customers in the door and pulls out their hard-earned cash. From the farmer's market end of things, discounting does have a couple advantages:

- It increases your revenue per customer
- It moves more product
- The customer is excited about a deal (how could you not get 2 jars?)
- It increases the chances they give away the other jars to other people.

You don't have to give a discount. Some small businesses are anti-discount. And I can see why. You want top-dollar for your hard work. The beauty of being small is you can experiment with your pricing. Give a deal one weekend - see what happens. Raise your prices, give a jar away for free with the purchase of 4 jars. Find what works and run with it.

With pricing figured out, how much product should you bring?

How much product should I bring?

I am notorious for screwing this up. Sometimes I don't bring enough. Other times, I bring WAY too much. And other times, I sell out of flavors. You never know. But, here are a couple tips to figure out how much product to bring:

1. Ask vendors

You'd be surprised at how much people are willing to reveal. I know a couple vendors' sales numbers at the market. It equates to the product they bring. For one, you don't want to schlep a ton of product back to your car. And on the other, you don't want to sell out. Ask vendors with some experience under their belt.

2. Bring more of your best sellers

If you haven't sold before, think of what your family and friends raved about -- bring more of that. We have a lot of flavors of mustard -- 11 at its max. Some we don't even bring to the market. Others we bring a case or two. And the rest (our top 4) we bring a good amount of.

FOODTRUCKEMPIRE

3. Estimate how much you'll sell

Find out how many people attend the farmer's market in a given week. You could estimate that around 5% of these people will be exposed to your booth and its products. And it's likely 1/3 of those people buy your product (if you have good selling skills -- coming up!). Then multiply that by an average purchase of 1-2 units and you have your estimated stock. Keep in mind, that's your sell-out stock. Add an extra 10% so you don't run out.

4. Is there an event going on?

I don't have to tell you this, but events in your city bring multiple things including people and their tourist dollars. They're on vacation and want to spend money on something unique from the area. The farmer's market is the perfect solution. Bring more product if there's an event going on in your town.

When do I need to get there?

I give myself two hours before the market starts. That means we get to the park at 6:30am for an 8:30am start. Sure, a couple vendors think we're crazy, but we get there when the big farms get there. It's a stress-free setup situation. There's no rush and it gives you time to run home if you forgot something.

If it's your first time, get there early.

Leave time to talk with the Market Manager to get the lay of the land, find your space, and follow directions to unload. The last you want is to pull your hair out trying to get setup in 30 minutes or less. Oh, and you definitely do not want to be late. Just like school, there's probably an attendance policy.

What if it's raining/bad weather?

Stop complaining, get in your car, and go to the market. Showing up when it's raining shows your dedication to the farmer's market, your loyal customers, and any new customers you may meet that morning. Plus, if you didn't go, you'd miss out on whatever money you would have made. We still make $200-$300 when it's raining. And that's nothing to shake a stick at.

Will everything fit in the car?

This is where things could get tricky. Don't get a car just because you got accepted into your local farmer's market - that's crazy talk! Work with what you have. You may not be able to fit a big white tent in your car. That's why a lot of people strap their tent to the roof. Grab some bungees and do the same.

 FOODTRUCKEMPIRE

Packing your setup into a small car forces you to think.

We drive a Honda Odyssey to large events. Yes, we have a soccer mom van, but it's the most comfortable ride that carries 1,200 pounds of mustard. But, when we added a 2nd or 3rd event to the weekend, everything had to suddenly fit into a Honda Accord. Miraculously, it does.

Constraints force you to think creatively. What do you absolutely have to bring to the market? Can you leave anything behind? This exercise helps you fit everything into your car, no matter what make and model.

Do I need any help?

Help comes in two forms: hired help and non-hired help (family & friends). I've used both to help me sell at events - and they both have pros and cons.

But first, why would you need help?

- You may not be able to do everything yourself
- It may be a large event
- You might be out of town
- You might have multiple events happening

For me, I'll take any help I can get setting up and breaking down our display. The faster I get those activities done, the better. Usually, my parents help out (who have stepped up in a big way this year). I've also had friends make deliveries and come to give me bathroom breaks. (You know you have awesome friends when they stop by just to let you run to the bathroom).

Really, this section is about hired help. You can get tons of free help (or product donation help), but when you have to hire help, it's a whole different ball game. I'll touch on the pros and cons of hired help at the farmer's market here and get into more detail about hiring a sales team later in the book.

Pros of hiring help at the farmer's market

1. You don't have to be there

There's a million other things you could be doing. Tasks you've been trying to complete for weeks probably. When you hire help, suddenly you get a chance to plow through your never-ending to-do list. And don't worry about your salesperson. They're an adult and will figure things out on their own. If something goes wrong, they'll call.

2. You get a fresh perspective

My salesperson was full of ideas. Ideas to sell more mustard. Ideas to get more retailers. And he'd pitch them all to me. When you operate your business all by yourself, you get used to "business as usual". When you bring someone in to help, you get a fresh set of eyes on what you never realized was a problem. While I had my salesperson, it was nice to not be the only one thinking about what's going on in the day-to-day.

3. You get a little bit of life back

Getting demos and a couple markets off my plate helped me get my life back. I was able to finally see some friends, go on a road-trip for the weekend, and get back to reading & writing. Hiring help when you need it is a chance to bring back the work- life balance everyone craves.

Cons of hiring help at the farmer's market

1. Lack of knowledge

This is the worst con. Even if you train them well, give them cheat sheets, and ask questions yourself, your salesperson is almost always going to be ill-prepared (compared to you). This makes your company appear weak. But, you don't know this happens unless your salesperson talks to you about it. That means open communication is essential if you choose to bring a new team member on.

2. A salesperson is not the owner

The best person to sell your product is you. No question. When people ask "do you make it?" and the response is anything other than "yes or I do" or "I'm the owner", they retract. It's strange and I'm still trying to understand why this happens. Businesses grow and need employees, but at something like a farmer's market, the owner is expected to be there 100% of the time. I've had customers tell me they didn't buy mustard from me because it wasn't me or my Dad under the tent. Crazy!

3. It can get expensive

Every farmer's market or event you pay someone to do adds to the overall cost of the event. I paid my salesperson $80 plus 5% commission on sales. While he only did a couple of farmer's markets for me, he also did several demos a month. This added up to a couple hundred dollars a month that, while beneficial, wasn't generating the return I needed to keep my salesperson (mainly because of reason 1 and 2).

 FOODTRUCKEMPIRE

4. It may create more work for you

When I hired my salesperson, I thought it'd lighten the load. Nope. I got more work. I had to manage his activities (I also had him doing some store demos), make sure he had everything, and then do the grunt work when he was back from events. While the pros above were nice, this was definitely a con.

Don't hire help right off. You're into your first farmer's market. This is your baby. You still have a lot to learn. And it's best you talk with customers first. You'll learn what they like, don't like, and even love. This is valuable feedback to help grow your business when you're just starting out.

And finally, the inevitable question...

What if I don't sell anything?

It's going to happen. It's happened to me before. I remember the day I sold less than $100 at a craft fair. I was selling an overpriced product in a blue-collar area. Customers simply couldn't spend $7 for a jar of mustard when they could get one for 99 cents in the grocery store.

If you don't sell anything don't get discouraged.

I've seen many food products launch at farmer's markets and disappear the next year. Not selling enough of your product is not a fun position to be in, but there are some strategies to help you produce a product line your customers clamor for:

1. Ask your customers

I ask people all the time why they buy the mustard they buy. I ask because I want to know who my competition is. And I get a lot of answers - from people who can't shut up about their favorite small-batch mustard to people who only eat the bright yellow stuff. Ask your market what they'd change about your product to make it better.

2. Come with multiple products

If you're testing the waters with a couple products, bring them all to your first couple markets because one product may sell better than the others. And that's when you pare back and focus on what's selling. Don't make your products because you want to make them. Make them because customers want to buy them.

3. Try another venue

This may sound funny, but we don't do well at events in New Hampshire (probably because we're from Vermont :p). So, we've tried other venues -- farmer's markets, festivals, fairs, long

 FOODTRUCKEMPIRE

ones, short ones. Maybe farmer's markets aren't the right venue for your product. Sure, you expose your product to thousands of people, but if they're not buying, go somewhere else.

4. Test Pricing

As I mentioned above, the beauty of owning a small business is having the ability to test your pricing. See what tips the scale -- maybe it's $1 less - or, maybe it's more expensive (believe it or not, it could work in your favor).

The Farmer's Market Essentials List

The resources section has a Farmer's Market Essentials List -- everything you need to make sure your first farmer's market goes off without a hitch. Basically, it's a list I bring with me to make sure everything is in the car.

10 Must-do's at your first farmer's market

Your display is set. You've got your cash box, tent, and packaging squared away. Now, it's time to hop in the car and experience your first farmer's market from the other side of the table. Here are ten must-do's when you get to your first farmer's market:

1. Introduce yourself to the Market Manager

This person runs the whole show - and quite frankly, isn't paid enough. Make sure you introduce yourself to him/her and show your appreciation for being at the market. Every hello & goodbye means a lot to the manager. Plus, they know where your spot is :)

2. Make friends with your neighbors

Make an effort to say hello to your neighbors - on both sides. Introduce yourself, let them know what you sell, and show an interest in their business. Building up these relationships not only helps you in the long run, but when you need that bathroom break, you'll know who to turn to.

3. Walk the market before it opens (carry your cash!)

If you've got a couple minutes of down-time, walk the market. Do this to see how other people get setup, what systems they use, and how they display their products. Get ideas out of your head and onto paper when you get back. Introduce yourself to more vendors, too. The more people who know you, the more they can refer their own customers to you. (Networking!) Oh, and don't forget to take your cash with you.

4. See if there are vendors you could partner with

While you're walking around, see who you could give product to to enhance or support their products. For example, we partner with a soft pretzel vendor and a sausage vendor. We give them free mustard and get free food (or product) back in return. Plus, it's a great way to drive traffic to our booth from the other side of the market. Who can you partner up with?

5. Find where the bathroom is

Oh, the bathroom. Sometimes (like when it's raining) you'll actually get to go to the bathroom. Other times, you'll learn how to not drink or eat anything, and avoid the sprint to the bathroom. But, you should at least know where it is to minimize time away from your tent.

6. Talk to as many potential customers as possible

If this is your first market, simply start talking to customers -- even if they don't buy your product. Get to know them, why they come to the market, why they're buying your product, and get feedback. What could make it better? What retailers could they see it on the shelf in?

7. Follow the market guidelines

Breaking the rules may have been cool in high school, but there's often guidelines in place at the market for a reason. Make sure you follow them to a T. You'll start to notice some are lax - and they should be -- but others are strictly enforced. And the last thing you want is to be out of the market with nowhere to sell your product. Pay attention - and if you have employees, make sure they know the rules, too.

8. Make it known you're new

When I was first starting out, I let all of my potential customers know I was new, just trying out a couple recipes, and I wanted their feedback. If they bought, cool -- if not, there is plenty of time to convert them into a customer! And customers love when they find something new. Then they go tell their friends and family. Don't you love word of mouth (literally)?

9. Make a list of what could have gone better

I can pretty much guarantee your first market is going to be a learning experience. Take note of everything going wrong and right. Find solutions to your problems for next time and everything will go much smoother. With a couple markets under your belt, you'll be a pro!

10. Thank the Market Manager

Sure, you may just be filling someone's spot on a rainy Saturday, but thank the Market Manager for the opportunity to bring your products to market. If you see him/her in person, do it then. If not, send a quick email the day after.

Bonus: Bring your health permit! The health inspector can do surprise inspections any day of the week -- and if you don't have your permit (yes, a simple piece of paper) they can shut you down. Make copies to keep everywhere - it'll get you out of a jam eventually!

Farmer's markets are a community. People -- organizers, vendors, and customers -- are there to help each other out. They care about the market and want to see it succeed. You are now a part of that community.

Now, that you're "in", let's talk about how you can take your 10x10 space at the market to the next level.

The next few sections teach you how to take advantage of your space at the farmer's market and launch the food business you've always dreamed of.

10 Ways to sell more at the farmer's market

1. Approach people

The farther you are away from people, the less likely they'll come to you. Heck, they may not even come near your tent. That's a problem. The second someone even glances at your booth, say "Hi! How are you".

They'll either get freaked out if you see them looking at your products or it'll be an opportunity to strike up a conversation. Why start with "How are you?" Because it's not a simple yes/no answer (this makes it an easy exit for people). It shows you're friendly and approachable. And they'll likely ask "What are you selling? " (even if it's obvious). This is your time to strike -- go pitch your new customer!

2. Partner with other vendors

As I mentioned a few times already, partnerships with other vendors can pay off. But, you have to do them right. Make sure you've got a sign at the other vendor's booth advertising your company, products, and location at the market. Your "partner" isn't going to have time to turn and point to where you are, so make a small sign and print it off at Staple of OfficeDepot.Do not hand-write one because that's not professional. Plus it reflects poorly on your "partner" if all his signs are printed.

3. Raise your prices

What? Yes. Raise your prices. It costs money to attend a farmer's market. You have to cover your overhead. In 2010 when we started selling mustard, it was $4 to the consumer. Now, it's $7. The cost of doing business is rising. And your loyal customers won't bat an eyelash at the

increased price if they understand you've got to cover your costs. While you may not sell as much product when you raise your prices, you bring in more money.

4. Frequent Buyer Cards

There's an old business saying - "80% of your revenue comes from 20% of your customers". This might not be right for farmer's markets because you get new customers each weekend. But, for your local (and loyal) customers, frequent buyer cards are one of the best ways to get customers coming back - especially if you start the card for them with a free punch! To get frequent buyer cards you can design them yourself or get them printed on Vistaprint. If you're looking for a mobile app, check out this list of mobile options.

5. Add another product line

I know more products can make setting up your display more complicated, but they could help you increase sales. For example, if you can jams, maybe you could sell pickles, relish, or salsa too. More product lines means your customers have a chance to try something different - a lot. But, beware: too many products can cause decision paralysis and your customers won't purchase anything because they can't make up their mind. Just look at this jam study.

6. Build better relationships

Your customers are people, too -- so treat them like so. I have met some amazing customers at the Burlington Farmer's Market. Some have even become friends - and most have become loyal customers. Give a discount every once in a while, give them access to exclusive flavors, or just say thank you for their continued support.

7. Encourage retail sale during the week(end)

If you're in a couple local retailers (which I'll get into in the next section), let your customers know so they can increase your sales during the week (or weekend, depending when your farmer's market is). While this doesn't increase market sales, it increases and encourages retail sale, which is more sustainable than market sales. (People go to the grocery store a few times a week -- and they won't go the market when it's raining)

8. Drive people to your website

If you do a market with a lot of tourists, they'll be out of your products a couple weeks after they get home. Make it easy for them to get to your website and order online. The Burlington Farmer's Market is loaded with tourists. That's why I've stopped giving out business cards. Now, I give out cards that promote our social media profiles and purchasing mustard online.

9. Launch limited edition flavors

I've been launching limited edition flavors for the past two years -- some stick around for three months -- some it's just a couple weeks. But, it creates scarcity. Since it's only going to be here for a limited amount of time, customers "feel" the need to purchase immediately - or it'll run out. This tactic is fun for you and your customers because they keep coming back to see if you've made something new.

10. Online advertising

While often the most expensive way to increase sales, it could work for your local market. Simply run a Facebook ad (more on that later, too) and target the town your market is in. Announce new flavors, reminders to shop for birthdays, holidays, etc. It exposes people to your brand who aren't customers and gives a gentle nudge to customers who already purchase your products.

With the tips in tow to increase your farmer's market sales, it's time to reveal the best way to increase your sales: improving your personal selling skills.

Personal selling is arguably the most essential skill to improve - at markets, retailers, and talking in general. Here are a couple ways you can turn simply talking to people into cold-hard cash.

13 Ways to improve your personal selling

1. Never sit down

Confident salespeople never sit down and read the newspaper. No one will approach your table if you do that. But, if you stand up, open your body position, and smile, customers will come flocking.

2. Compliment your customers

Compliments (especially with female customers) go a long way in business - even if you fake it until you make it. Compliment jewelry, handbags, etc. You'll get a smile and hopefully a sale!

3. Find common ground

Look at your customer's hats and sweatshirts. Do you recognize the place? If so, strike up a conversation. Or, simply ask a question like "Where are you from?" or "Are you in town for the weekend". Your investment in getting to know your potential customers makes you more friendly and approachable. And when you're approachable, customers are more likely to buy from you.

 FOODTRUCKEMPIRE

4. Say Thank You

When I've purchased from other farmer's market vendors, many of them have not said thank you. Crazy, right? Say thank you! Look your customers directly in the eye and thank them for their business. You know they can spend their money elsewhere, so thank them for spending it with you on your products.

5. Remember Your Customer's Name

Loyal customers are my favorite. They not only support my business, but in some cases they've become friends. One way to take your customer relationship to the next level is to simply remember their name. It's that easy. They'll feel like they're part of something - and you appreciate their business.

6. Be Natural

Don't sound salesy. Be relaxed. "What's going on guys?" or "How's it going this morning". Be yourself. Take a deep breath. You're just dealing with human beings. It's not a job interview. Strike up random conversations and see where it goes. Often, they buy from you just because you're a neat person. "I'm going to buy from you because I like you" is easily one of the best compliments you can get.

7. Customer First

If customers need a bag to hold their other purchases, offer it to them – even if they don't buy from you – it's all about customer service (plus, it draws them into your booth). Fill your bags with marketing materials like recipes and business cards. That way, even if their bag is full of other products, they'll be reminded of your brand when they get home and unpack.

8. Assess Your Body Language

Body language is everything. Try not to cross your arms. Don't sit down or be on your phone. That doesn't create a welcoming booth. Smiling and eye contact are powerful, too. Sometimes, I even do jumping jacks to stay warm (Vermont is 30 degrees in the morning in May and October). The motion attracts people and brings them into my booth (oh, and I burn off the scone I had for breakfast).

9. Find Common Ground & Tell Stories

People like forming relationships with you. Ask questions about a location on their shirt or hat. Ask what they might be doing in town, where they are from. Take an interest in them – don't even try to sell them anything – and all of a sudden you'll notice you've opened up a pretty nice sales opportunity. Go get 'em!

10. Paint a Picture

Some customers might need some help imagining how they're going to use your products. Paint a picture for them. Here's an example for college students who want to know what our mustard goes well with: This mustard goes great on grilled cheese.

Get some aged-cheddar and crunchy sourdough. It all just melts together into one gooey mess. So, so good. Are you thinking about grilled cheese now?

11. Be Confident

You'll sell a lot more if you know you can sell it. Pump yourself up at the beginning of the day and in the middle. Don't let a no-sale let you down. Get the next guy :p

12. Sell What Sells

If you know what moves, sell more of that. Or, sell your favorite. While there are flavors for everyone, sell what brings in the money. And as I'm sure you've experienced, you'll only sell what you sample. Sample three flavors but have ten? Bring more of what you sell. Plus, be prepared to sample everything when a customer asks about that mystery jam on your shelf.

13. Have a Reason to Come Back

Why should customers come back to you next week? This is why we have the test lab flavors. It gets people coming back week after week to see what's new (or to stock up). Plus, they enjoy talking to you. If you can, try to learn their name, too. Using names in conversation shows you care about your customers. Yes, it's a lot of work. but it makes a HUGE difference.

How to analyze your farmer's market performance

How are you performing at the market?

It's time for analysis.

If numbers freak you out, you've got to get used to them. You can't come back from the market thinking what you made is what's in your cashbox. That's not realistic - and your business will crumble if you don't know the exact number.

Here's how I analyze each farmer's market:

Step 1: Write down what you're bringing before the market on an index card or piece of printer paper. (This includes cash, too)

 **FOODTRUCK**EMPIRE

You have to know what you brought. That way you know what you sold at the end of the day. Keep track of what products you're bringing to the market as well as the cash in your cash box. I like to keep a stack of index cards under my money to make sure there's always one handy.

Step 2: Use the other side of the card to take notes

I don't know about you, but I write down a lot at the farmer's market. Whether it's different mustards people enjoy, retailers they'd love to see our product in, or a supplier's name from another vendor, the notes are how you make connections to grow your business. Keep the back-side of your note card blank so you can keep notes during the market.

Step 3: Keep track of what you open to sample out or barter (if you do)

I'm still trying to keep a better track of this myself. When you crack a jar open to sample, write it down. Why? It costs you money. Samples expense is it's own line on my income statement so I can see how much I'm sampling out at different events or to retail buyers. And if you barter for humus, nut butter, meat or eggs, right that down, too -- not just "one jar" but the flavor as well because all of your products have different costs.

Step 4: Write down your ending inventory (minus samples) when you get home

Just as you did at the beginning, write down the inventory you're bringing home. Add the samples back in and you have the number of units you sold at the farmer's market.

Step 5: Count your money

One of my favorite things to do is count the twenty dollar bills at the end of the market because they are all on their way to my bank account, of course! Make sure to count checks, credit card transactions, and any alternative forms of payment (market-funded tokens for example).

Step 6: Find your price / unit (if possible)

If you sell one product line (like 9 oz jars of mustard), you can find your price per unit. This is especially useful if you use tiered discounting or need to see if your cash or inventory may be off. It also tells you if you sold more single jars or if people bought multiple jars at a better price.

Step 7: File any notes you took into a Google Docs

Remember those notes you took in step 3? Type them up into a Google Doc that serves as a to-do list for you if you need to follow up with anything or anyone you ran into today. And remember to hammer away at the document weekly -- those sales leads only stay hot for so long!

You can sign up for Google Docs for free at docs.google.com.

 FOODTRUCKEMPIRE

Step 8: Generate a market-only profit and loss statement

With multiple streams of revenue over the course of the year, it's hard to identify the impact your farmer's market has had on sales, operating expenses and profit. That's why you need to extract sales and inventory data to discover how much money you actually made this market season. This may require an accountant or you can do it manually, too.

Step 9: Find your top-selling products

One of the best data points you can get from doing a farmer's market is top-selling products. This helps you sell more product to other market customers. Plus, it's useful information to have when you're speaking with buyers who are looking for a rank of your product line.

Step 10: Write down a list of ways you can improve for next season.

Our sales strategy and display could always use improvement,

Bonus Step: Analyze your performance against the market's overall performance

Can you tell I'm a numbers geek, yet? Our farmer's market sends out categorized numbers for all vendors a couple months after the market season ends to compare against previous years. You can use this data, too, to compare your own company.

- Did you stay on trend with the market?
- When were your better days (or worse days) better than the market's?

What percentage of sales were you in your category?

These questions help gauge if you're "just another vendor" or performing "exceptionally well" and help you plan for next year's market.

And that's the end of the farmer's market guide.

There's a lot to learn about your own farmer's market -- they aren't all the same. Find out what makes your stand work and do more of it. If it's a new display, training your sales team, or partnering up with other vendors, seek ways to increase your sales. This information is only to serve as a reference and a "starter guide" if you will.

You now have the resources to make great money at the farmer's market. Best of luck with the upcoming season!

What's next in the guide?

Finding your first few retailers - and getting your product on the shelf!

The grocery industry is rooted in distribution. Your goal is to get your product in as many stores as possible - that's called distribution. With increased distribution comes product cost improvements, potential to hire staff, and of course increased sales.

Traditionally, companies have been successful with a retail strategy because grocery stores are the first place customers discover new items. It's typically not online, and it could be at events, but grocery stores are the best ways to achieve sustainable growth for your company.

Over the next few sections, I'll explore everything there is to getting your product into retail, including:

- How to find retailers & make sure you're not wasting your time.
- How to price correctly for retail & the effects of discounting
- How to prepare for your first buyer's meeting
- How to scale your retail strategy
- How to demo and improve your same-store sales
- Working with brokers
- Working with distributors
- Meeting buyer's demands
- How to self-distribute
- Personal lessons I've learned working in retail

And, of course, there's a whole lot more, too. Let's get started! Retail is likely going to be a significant driver to your business's top line, so take notes.

Before we get into the meat of grocery retail, I'd like to talk about why retail works for your business - and why it may not. It's not the right strategy for everyone.

Why retail works for the food industry

1. It's where consumers shop

You probably go to the grocery store once or twice a week, right? And you purchase similar groceries each week, but maybe try a couple new products. That's how food businesses survive - your risk to try new products. Then, when you love it, you make their product part of your routine purchases. Know they know where to get your item. The trick is getting it into the right

FOODTRUCKEMPIRE

grocery stores where your customers shop.

2. There are a ton of them

There are 37,459 grocery stores that gross over $2Million (FMI). In addition to the 45,997 specialty food stores you're likely to target when starting out (IBIS). That's an enormous market. And it provides you the opportunity to get a small chunk of market share to build your successful food company,

3. A couple large accounts can build a big business

You could land a couple large accounts and build a successful business. With a high turn product, you may only need a handful of retailers for a livable income. But, we all know you want to grow. And you're always going to be looking for larger stores. Those big accounts with grocery stores can make (or break) your company.

Why retail doesn't work for the food industry

1. Your margins diminish

Large grocery stores are not high-end gourmet specialty shops. That's why if your product is distributed to both, there could be a $3 discrepancy between the price on the shelf at both stores. Then, with grocery stores, they expect your product to run on promotion for a certain part of the year -- and that cost comes from your pocket. All of a sudden, you're making 25 cents or less on each unit. That's a lot of product to sell to put food on the table. I've learned the hard way.

2. You may not live in an area with large grocery chains

I live in rural Vermont. The closest Whole Foods Market is 3 hours away. That makes it expensive for me to sell into Whole Foods. While there are large independent grocery stores, large chains (where retail growth really is) are at a distance. If you're in the same place, I'll help you strategize later in this chapter.

3. Your product could be kicked off the shelf at anytime

There's a reason large food manufacturers (Kraft, P&G, etc) rule the grocery store. They want your shelf space. And they'll do anything in their power to get it. It might mean acquiring brands like yours or paying to get your product off the shelf. The one thing to remember is that when you go on the shelf, it's likely another brand is coming off the shelf. It could be a big producer or a small producer. Remember your product's time on the shelf could be limited.

In summary, retail is a distribution strategy ripe with opportunity, but sprinkled with risk. It'll work well for you locally, but as you start to expand outside of your county or state, you may

encounter some resistance from the "other local ____ company" who has shelf space in retailers you'd like to be in.

Anyway, let's continue on into the world of retail.

How to find your first retailers

1. Don't look where you shop

Just because you shop at Whole Foods, Wegmans, Kroger, or another large grocery store doesn't mean it's the perfect test set of stores for your food product. If you have the customer base and your product figured out, as well as an increased production capacity, then go for it. But, I'd encourage you to seek out smaller stores first. These stores hold your hand through the beginning stages to make sure you have everything worked out when you do approach larger stores.

2. Select high traffic locations

Your hometown could be pretty tiny (mine is!). This means you've got to find higher traffic retailers to sell your product. Head into the city and explore small coops, specialty food stores, etc. You want locations that send thousands of customers through the checkout line daily.

3. Select locations with high tourist traffic

Tourists are likely to be a large part of your retail presence in the beginning. They're looking for something made in the area they're visiting. Plus, they're willing to spend more than your average customer. Even though you might not like going to the tourist traps in your area, do it for the business.

4. Start with stores where the buyer is easily accessible

Smaller stores love to work with smaller producers. After all, you've got to get your start somewhere, right? When I started, I worked with a handful of small coops, directly with buyers, to bring my product in. As we grew, I had the confidence to approach bigger buyers. One helpful buyer when you launch your product can be the difference between your company rocketing to success or crashing and burning.

5. Ask your test market

If you did test marketing of your products using the process in a previous chapter, you'll know exactly where to sell your product. And if you haven't, it isn't too late. Call up your friends and family and ask, "Where would you purchase my product? Where do you see it being purchased?"

Start with a list of 3-5 retailers. Don't go all in contacting hundreds of retailers because you still need to prove your concept -- product-market fit, if you will. You need to know customers support your product before you expand into 20, 50, 100 retailers. Otherwise, it's going to be a money-suck of an adventure.

Before you head into the stores to pitch your product, there's a ton of prep to do. You have to show you know what you're talking about - and can talk the talk of the industry - before your product ends up on the shelf.

Let's get started:

What you need before you approach a buyer

1. FDA-compliant packaging

There is a lot that MUST go on your label -- and it could be different for each state. For example, some states require you state your product is made in a home kitchen. Some require a business ID number, too. Since labels are a large cash expense, make sure all of this is correct. Get your labels approved by your state's Agency of Agriculture before you send them to the printer.

2. A Sell Sheet (more on what's included in the next couple pages)

Sell sheets are advertisements for your company's products. They help you tell a story -- how you got started, why your products stand out, and how your line is represented. No need to make these extra special. Simply communicate information and have beautiful photos because they get recycled anyway.

3. Price of Your Product

Many buyers are price conscious, so know your numbers. How much you sell it for, what the case price is, and what the MSRP (manufacturer's suggested retail price) is. This helps the buyer gauge where your line lands among the other products on the shelf.

4. UPC codes

When you're starting your food company, it's always a big debate whether or not to invest in barcodes. Getting real barcodes is expensive, which is why many food producers opt for recycled barcodes, I'll get into the difference a little later in this section.

 FOODTRUCKEMPIRE

5. Business cards

Business cards are passe, but they serve a different purpose for a buyer vs. if you're at a networking event. When I was getting started, my business cards were magnetic. It had my contact information on it and prompted the buyer to call if they needed more mustard.

6. List of distributors with item numbers

If you're doing sales calls on behalf of your distributor, bring along the item information so they can easily order your product line without having to search through your distributor's catalog.

7. Promotion plan (optional)

Are you going to run a summer promotion? Maybe a holiday sale? Let the buyer know up-front that you'd like to work with the promotions team to move more product throughout the year. Sale signs attract people to your products on the shelf and encourage product trials - that's exactly what you want!

8. Point of sale (optional)

Generally, stores operate on a "clean-store policy". That means they only use their specific signage and do not allow point-of-sale materials like a postcard that attaches to the shelf -- often called a shelf-talker. If you have point-of-sale printed, bring it to show the buyer. If it's not accepted, don't let that make or break the relationship you're building.

9. Ordering information

How does the buyer get your product? Here's a quick bulleted list of what the buyer needs to know:

- Contact information & who to talk to.

- Case-pack size (how many units come in a case)

- Minimum order

How you get the product there (direct delivery, shipping, distributor)

10. Your product's ranking (optional)

Ranking is needed if you have more than 4 sku's in your product line. I've had to send over my product's ranking a handful of times. It helps buyers purchase what they know will sell. Keep in mind your product's ranking in the northeast is going to be different than in the south or west coast. And if you have recently introduced items, make note of that on your ranking, too.

11. An appointment

I used to spring myself on buyers -- unannounced. I hated it. And they probably hated it more. Now, I try my best to schedule appointments or give the buyer a heads up that I'll be coming in on Tuesday morning. Appointments show professionalism and respect for the buyer's time. Make a great first impression by scheduling your time with the buyer.

12. Confidence & a positive attitude

You can't go into a sales meeting knowing you're going to fail. Have confidence in your product line. You have come this far already. It's only the beginning of your journey. People love your products already, so why won't a retailer?

Out of everything on that list, the sell sheet is most confusing. Let's tackle that one first.

How to make a sell sheet for your food business

Sell sheets are essential to landing new retail accounts – especially when you're sending blind samples to a buyer. Read on to find out how to make one for your food business.

Want to impress buyers and land more retail accounts?

Ding-ding-ding! Every food business wants to do that. And it starts with sell sheets. Sell sheets are the advertising of the specialty food industry. They show off your product, provide ordering information, and often are the first thing to cross a buyer's desk (hopefully with samples).

But creating an awesome sell sheet isn't easy.

There's so much to cram on there, it's hard to make it look pretty and communicate what your brand is all about. Plus, awesome sell sheets tend to be designed by expensive branding agencies. And as a small food business, you don't have the money to pay a designer.

That means you probably need to go the do-it-yourself route: Make your own sell sheet. And that's what this blog post is attempting to accomplish. Here's what you'll learn:

- What goes on a sell sheet?
- 5 great examples of sell sheet?
- How do I design a good sell sheet?
- Ready to learn how to make a sell sheet for your food business?

Let's get started with what actually goes on a sell sheet.

 FOODTRUCKEMPIRE

There are certain things that should go on a sell sheet. Below you'll find a list of ten suggested parts of your sell sheet.

What should go on a sell sheet?

1.Contact information

I'll start with the obvious. Add your name, address, phone number, email (and fax if you have it) to your sell sheet. And don't just include a business card – those get lost. Having your contact information in more than one place assures the buyer they'll be able to find it.

2. Big "money-shot" picture

Think about what draws you in to look at something – it's the visuals. And the same is true with your sell sheet. Have product photography at the ready so you have some variety in what picture you're going to choose. In the examples below, you'll notice how beautiful photography plays a key role in selling.

3. Your product line

How many products do you have? While you don't have to go into detail for each product, list your different varieties – and note your most popular products. If buyers have to limit the number of SKUs they bring in, they want to know what's going to move best. Note buzz-words, too, like gluten-free, dairy-free, etc.

4. UPC's (if you have room)

Why put ugly barcodes on your sell sheet? If your products get accepted, the buyer needs these to add to their inventory system. An alternative is to list the UPC codes in a table – that way you have more room for everything else on this list.

5. Customer testimonials

Customers LOVE your product. Retailers want to see that their customers will, too. Testimonials are powerful tools to show buyers your product is tops in the market. 2- 3 is a good number – you don't want to go overboard!

6. List of distributors

How are retailers going to get your product? Sure, you may deliver directly to retailers, but sometimes it's easier for buyers to order everything through one distributor.

7. Ordering details

Do you have order minimums? Do you ship? What about mixing cases? If you answer all these questions on your sell sheet, you'll be closer to getting an order because the buyer won't have to clarify anything with you.

8. What makes you different

This should be higher on the list, but what you're ultimately trying to do is convince the buyer that your jam (or mustard, brownies, etc) are better than other products. Do you have a unique story? Are your ingredients local? What about your flavors – are they like nothing ever seen before?

9. Pricing

Another obvious one. List your pricing – by unit and case. Don't hide it or make the buyer call. And make sure to have separate distributor and wholesale pricing (but don't list them on the same sell sheet).

10. Your story

Food is all about the people who make it – what's your story? Sure, you may not be a 15-year-old kid or an aspiring chef, but everyone has a story. Make it come through on your sell sheet.

And it's as simple as that. While some of this is optional (I don't include everything here on my sell sheet for Green Mountain Mustard), feel free to customize your company's sell sheet to your needs.

So, what's next?

Well, I figured I'd give you a few examples of well-designed sell sheets. Let's look at five I've come across on my foodie travels (including mine!).

What do great sell sheets look like?

1. Green Mountain Mustard (yep – this is mine!)

Link: https://cdn.shopify.com/s/files/1/0322/1197/files/GMM_SellSheet_FINAL.pdf?1099

2. Kayem Brats Grilling Sausage (bold design – great branding)

Link: http://i.imgur.com/Z9sSZ.png

3. Spice Mama (awesome example of how to display a big product line)

Link: https://www.pinterest.com/pin/497084877617488594/

Aren't these great sell sheets? I tried to showcase different products and strategies used to make these sell sheets pop. Now, you're probably wondering: "How do I make my sell sheet amazing?" It just so happens I've got a couple tips for you.

> # I make the best food ever.
>
> Strawberry
> —Jam—
>
> $5.99/jar

Want to get a beautiful sell sheet for your food business? You'll find a few tips below!

How do you get a great-looking sell sheet?

1. Use a template

A lot of food businesses try to scrap together a sell sheet in Microsoft Word and it almost never comes out the way you want it to. That's why I suggest using a template. Look around Canva.com for inspiration. This website will help you a lot with all sorts of design needs. It's also cheap and easy to use. You can also Google "Sell Sheet Examples" for all sorts of inspiration from top consumer brands.

2. Take great photography

Seems to always end up that great photography sells everything. Simply put, it does. If you're not a pro at food photography, here are a couple of sites and eBooks that may help you out. Or, get the professionals to do it!

– Tasty Food Photography

– PhotographingFood

– An Introduction to Food Photography

3. Have a plan

Open up Microsoft Word or Photoshop and all you see is a blank screen. Well, clearly that's not going to help you! Instead, grab a sketch pad and draw out what you want your sell sheet to look like. See what photos and text you need and fill in where necessary. Sketch a couple of ideas out. That way when you go to create your sell sheet, you have a few options to choose from.

4. Don't be afraid to call in the pros

Do-it-yourself sell sheets aren't easy. And some people are just better at making food than trying to make a sell sheet work. That's when you may want to consider bringing in a professional designer to help you create the look you want. Here are a few resources to find a freelance designer:

– DesignCrowd.com

– Fiverr.com - I use this website all the time! Designs cost a lot less than you might think.

– Your local high school or college design department (cool class project)

Sell sheets are your most important asset when trying to land new retail accounts. And getting a beautiful sell sheet is tough because there are so many working parts. Hopefully with these tips, you'll be well on your way to creating your first sell sheet.

With the sell sheet in hand, let's tackle UPC codes (since they should be part of your sell sheet).

Getting UPC Codes: GS1 vs. recycled

UPC Codes are a big decision. Both solutions -- recycled and GS1 -- have their advantages and disadvantages. Ultimately, it depends on where you want your business to go. Here's a look at why you'd choose each type of barcode.

Why you should choose recycled barcodes

1. They're inexpensive

100 barcodes costs you $45 at Nationwide Barcode. That's cheap compared to the GS1. As a startup, you can't go wrong, but you get what you pay for -- recycled barcodes. These aren't

FOODTRUCKEMPIRE

yours. An aspiring entrepreneur bought thousands of barcodes and is simply reselling them to small businesses.

2. You don't plan to sell to large grocery stores

If you want to make some extra cash selling a product to small retailers in your state, then you're probably fine with recycled barcodes. And some retailers may not even require them, so maybe you won't need them!

3. You don't mind them not being in sequence

Let's face it. Most entrepreneurs are type A. That means we like things in order. Unfortunately recycled barcodes (most of the time) don't come in order - you could have a different prefix, too - depending on when you buy barcodes and need more. That creates an inconsistency in the retailer's system. Plus, the global UPC record- keeping system is going to see your barcodes as someone else's -- whether it's an old product or not (that's what recycled barcoded are).

Why you should choose GS1 barcodes

1. Many large grocery stores require them

You can't step foot into large grocery stores like Wegmans, Harris Teeter, and EarthFare without GS1 barcodes. They have you provide your GS1 company prefix on your paperwork for new item submission. There's no way around it.

2. You get your OWN barcodes

I own my own prefix now -- specific to Green Mountain Mustard. That's pretty awesome. And no one else shares that prefix. That means when I have national distribution, I'll be able to look up sales data on my product -- that's data unavailable to me right now.

3. It's an investment

If you start a food company, you've got to be in for the long haul. That means making investments where you need to. One of those is real GS1 barcodes. They run $750 for 25 barcodes and then $150/year for "membership". **Make the investment.**

I started with recycled barcodes and made the switch to my own GS1 barcodes 3 years later. I've never looked back. It's helped my product on the shelf at larger retailers and made my company legitimate in the eyes of buyers. And it's made it a hassle to get my barcodes changed with older retailers.

Ultimately, it's your decision. **I'd recommend GS1 barcodes from the beginning.**

 FOODTRUCKEMPIRE

How to get your GS1 barcodes:

It's pretty simple. Head over to the GS1 and get started. (Note: I do not make a commision off this link. It's simply provided as a resource).

Next, I'd like to cover promotional plans. There's a lot of vocabulary you should be familiar with before you approach a buyer -- most of which is covered in this section on promotional plans.

How to make a killer promotional plan

The grocery industry practically runs on promotions. Why do you go through the circular ads every week to decide what to buy? Sale items drive you to purchase product. And that's what we're after as food producers. We want to move more product. Promotions do just that.

Let's explore them further.

This section is going to walk you through:

- Why you need a promotional plan

- What kinds of promotions you can run

- How much promotions cost

- How to measure your promotion

- Alternative ways to promote your product

Why you need a promotional plan

1. Grocery stores run on promotions

You are a victim of the grocery store's promotional calendar. You probably buy what's on sale any given week. Chicken one week, pork the next, ketchup, then bbq sauce. Sale items make people buy. That's why stores run them all the time. It gets people into the store. And it's worked for as long as I can remember.

2. You move more product

As with any promotion, you're going to move more product -- even if it's ten cents off. Moving product increases your customer trial. And your hope is to turn some of those initial trial customers into customers for life.

3. Access to new customers

With premium products, customers take risks trying new products every day. With a sale, the barrier to trial is psychologically lower, ultimately helping you attract customers who would not have tried your product. New customers = more sales. And who doesn't want that?

4. Test your pricing strategy

Pricing influences many decisions of your business - from sales, to gross profit margin, and more. And when you're small, you can test your pricing. Does more product move at $3.99 or $4.99. Test it out. One of those ways is to run a promotion. Sure, you run the risk of customers only buying when your product goes on promo, but if they love it that much, 50 cents is not going to make a difference.

5. Clear-out old product / You're getting new packaging

There was a period of time where I was selling old-labeled, one-year-shelf-life product. I had the new labels ready to go - 40,000 sitting in my basement. I ran a couple promotions at our best retailers, did a handful of demos, and cleared most of the old product. As of this writing, there are still jars flying around some small retailers, but it's almost all gone. This is a great reason to run a promotion.

There are a lot of benefits to running promotions. But, it's important to know.....

You don't have to do promotions.

Yes. That's right. Your product **never** has to go on sale. Obviously, promotions cost money. And when you're starting out, money is tight. You can wait until you get into retailers who are used to running promotions and other advertising. It's ok.

But, if you've decided to run promotions, read on. There's lots to learn to make sure you're still making money on every product sold.

What kind of promotions can you run?

There are a lot of different promotions to run in the grocery store. Here's a run-down of every promotion I've ever encountered:

Store Demos

Demos are the most popular part of the promotional plan. People LOVE to taste your products. And you need them to try your product in to buy. Plus, if you pitch to the buyer that you'll demo 4-6 times a year, they'll love you. Demo support is huge in your promotional plan.

Off-Invoice Promotions

Off-invoice promotions are taken directly, well, off your invoice when you send it to the buyer. Off-invoice (OI for short) promotions are run for a certain amount of time -- a month or a quarter -- in hopes your promotions hit the shelf and get your customer's attention.

What? You mean my promotions won't hit the shelf?

Yes. It is possible. You may discount your price just to get your product on the shelf - or move more product that's close to code - and your discount won't reach the consumer. That's why you should bring it up to the buyer that you'd like the discount to hit the shelf. Sometimes, stores require a minimum discount for this to happen - like a $1 off for example.

Hard-Line Promotions

If you manufacture one product line, chances are you'll find yourself doing a hard- line promotion. Hard-line promotions are where the discount gets applied to the entire product line - 10% off all mustard for the month of June, for example.

Seasonal Promotions

These promotions align with the highs in your sales cycle. For many food businesses, this means holiday time and the summer grilling months if you make sauces. Of course, you could also run promotions in the "off-season" months to drive sales.

Scan-Down Promotions

Scan downs are when you run a promotion and partner with the retailer to split (usually) the difference on the promotion on just the product that gets "scanned" at the register during a certain period.

For example, I ran a two-week scan-down for $0.40 with a retailer. During that time we sold 24 units. My share of the promotion was $0.25. That means the scan-down cost me $6.00. I try to run a couple scan-downs a year because they are quick. And there is not a lot of risk -- plus, you get to see how many units you sold during a certain period.

If retailers are looking to do a longer promotion, say for the month of July during BBQ season, they'll likely ask for an off-invoice promotion.

BOGO and "Two-for" Promotions

You see these "buy one get one free" promotions all the time with baked goods like bread, cookies, and other canned goods, too. They're incredibly effective..."But, honey, it's $2/7...we might as well get two!" I use this psychology with our customers at farmer's markets and festivals because it converts so well.

Coupons

Even though you can access coupons on your smartphone, consumers are still cutting coupons every time they head to the grocery store. And they're about 1% effective. That's because coupons (generally) are not effective in creating repeat purchases. But, you can still run them in flyers or work with stores directly to offer a coupon promotion. To do this, you'll want to work with a coupon clearing house like NCH (I don't have any experience in couponing, so work with them at your own risk).

Grocery Flyer Advertising

With large - and even some small - grocery stores sending weekly flyers to their communities, there's a prime opportunity to get your promotion in-front of thousands of potential customers. Sometimes, stores or distributors charge for this -- sometimes they don't. My mustard was on sale at a small store in Massachusetts and they advertised it for free! How cool is that? Know this won't happen often, though.

What are the best promotions?

After running a couple of promotions, here are my top 3 most-effective promotions:

1. Scan-downs that hit the shelf

Why? In many cases retailers help you cover the cost of the promotion. Plus, you only pay for the units run through the register during a certain timeframe. And they're way more effective when the promotion gets advertised to customers. Otherwise, why bother?

2. In-store demos, timed perfectly

Why? As I said above, you're bound to run store demos that don't move a lot of product. I've done plenty where I haven't moved more than 10 jars. But, more have been perfectly timed. Say, a sale at the store, event, or holiday where your product pairs perfectly. That's when you're product flies of the shelf. Here's an example: 20 jars in 3 hours Super Bowl Sunday. Yes, please.

 FOODTRUCKEMPIRE

3. Hard-line intro discounts

Why? Because they're easy. And it gives a reason for new retailers to pull in your product line. I've ran 10% hard-line intro discounts with many of my distributors, coupled with focused sales calls to their top accounts. It's a recipe for success.

How to gauge if promotions are working

Why run a promotion if you can't measure the effectiveness? It's important to know when something's not working because you have the chance to fix it. And you definitely don't want your promotions going downhill.

Here's how to make sure your promotion is on track: check the shelves

Feet on the ground. It's a tried and true approach. Sometimes I check shelves at retailers two to three times a week. After a holiday weekend, I like to see what's moved at my larger accounts in Vermont. If your promo spans a few weeks (or months), you can either talk with the buyer (see below) or monitor the self. It's a great way to see how it's going without having to bother the buyer.

Talk with the buyer/demo coordinator

Check in with the buyer (or demo coordinator if it's a large store) at the beginning of your demo (the cashier if it's a small store and you're sampling) and see what they recommend to make the promotion/sampling better. Then, when the promotion is finished ask for a report of the units sold - by flavor. This shows you how effective your demo was during a certain time period. Plus, it builds your relationship with the buyer. That's key when you want to introduce new skus into the system or get better shelf placement.

Talk with customers

At my last demo, I stumbled on six people who routinely purchase our mustard at the store I was sampling in. This was valuable information because I was able to see and talk to who my customer was. Were they older or younger? Did they appear affluent? Did they have kids with them? What were they using the mustard for? There are all sorts of questions to ask when you're staring your customer in the eye. Take advantage of a longer conversation if you have the time. You'll learn a ton.

Keep track of performance

It's so nice to have something to compare to from last month or last year. That way you can see if you're making progress, and what, if anything, made the promotion perform differently. You

can keep track of demo performance, scan-downs, and couponing -- all of it. In the resources section, you'll find a demo progress sheet you can use to track your progress.

What if your promotion fails?

It's true. You may not see a spike in sales. Heck, I've done demos where a whopping two jars of mustard have sold - in 4 hours. Clearly, I learned a few things after that one (find out what later!). But, you have to think about why you're running the promotion in the first place:

- You want more people to try your product
- You want current customers to buy more
- You want to build a relationship with retailers & distributors

Those are three solid reasons to run promotions. Plus, it could be anything that led your promotion awry....poor timing, competing category promotions, or not enough of a discount (hey, you can only give so much). You never know. That's what makes distributor and retailers follow-up so important.

Aren't there other ways to get people to buy my product?

I understand promotions may not be the best route for you to go -- especially if your margins don't allow for them. That means you need to find alternative ways to get customers into your retail accounts and purchase your products. Here are a few quick ideas (more marketing ideas are detailed later in the book when you learn about marketing your brand):

Facebook advertising: Run Facebook ads in cities where you have retailers. Downside is it's hard to track return on investment and can get expensive.

Throw a party: When you turn one (or three or five) years old, throw a party. Or maybe you want to throw a summer BBQ or potluck. Whatever it may be, make dishes you'd use your product in/on, and have fun, It doesn't have to be expensive. Oh, and include a list of area retailers where your attendees can find your product on the shelf.

Sponsor a menu item at a restaurant: I've given discounted mustard to a couple delis to put on their sandwiches. It's basically free publicity, and I get the entire sandwich-making team talking about my products -- plus, customers ask where they can but it..and...BAM! You have retail sales.

Sample your heart out: Although mentioned above already, it's basically free. Do as many demos as possible in the beginning. Find a small farmer's market (about $100 to enter), or sign up to sample at a beer, cheese, or holiday craft fair.

Basically, you want to do anything to get your product into as many (of the right) mouths as possible.

Pro tip: Increase your sampling allowance in the beginning. Give product to pretty much anyone. Ask for a review on their blog, a Facebook shout out, Youtube video, etc. Get your name out there. One of the cheapest ways to do that is to give your product away.

How to knock it out of the park with every buyer

With a promotional plan in place, it's time to hit the pavement and **get in front of the buyers** you chose in your store research a few pages ago.

Store meetings can be nerve-wracking. What's going to happen? Will they like me? What if I screw up?

Breathe.

The meeting doesn't have to make you nervous. That's why I developed a proven 5- step plan I use with every buyer. It takes 5-10 minutes and you're out the door. Simple enough, right?

5 Steps to convince the buyer your product should be on the shelf

With a super-premium product, I often have the challenge of convincing the buyer why my product is worthy of their limited shelf space. Here's the five step approach I use, whether I'm meeting with a buyer in person, over the phone, or a random encounter in the store.

Step 1: Give your 30-second pitch

Your pitch is useful beyond the retail buyer. You can use it at farmer's markets, your website, and with anyone who asks about your company (which should be a ton. I get asked in Costco almost weekly what I'm doing with all that garlic and/or vinegar).

How to build a 30-second pitch.

The best way is to start with a framework. I've included a worksheet for you at the end of the book where you can fill in the blanks and have a basic 30-second pitch in a couple minutes.

A basic pitch includes four sentences:

- Your name

- The product you make

- Why it's different (don't compete on price)

- Why the buyer's store is right for your product.

Here are a few examples:

Example 1: Mustard Company (mine)

"Hi! My name is Michael, and I own Green Mountain Mustard. Our product is a line of super-premium mustard made locally in Vermont. Our flavor combinations are like nothing you have on your shelf. And a lot of our customers at the farmer's market have been looking for a place to pick up our mustard during the week. I think your retailer would be an amazing fit."

Why this pitch works:

- Local company with proven demand
- Offering something not currently on the shelf
- Close with a compliment

Example 2: Brownie Company

"Hi! My name is Alexa. I own Bobbie's Brownies. Bobbie is my Grandmother who has been making brownies from her secret recipe for over 30 years and I'm bringing them to market. What makes them different is their size. We make one-square inch brownie bites packed with dense chocolate flavor. We have one sku right now which makes it perfect to test the market in your store with little up-front cost."

Why this pitch works:

1. Great story - family businesses always have awesome stories
2. Clear difference over other brownies on the shelf
3. One sku means less risk for the retailer up-front

Example 3: Potato Chip Manufacturer

"Hi! My name is Jim with Chip Off the Old Block. I've been making tortilla chips out of sweet corn

for a couple years in my house and have decided to sell them. Most mass-marketed chips are made with corn by-products. Ours is made with sweet corn grown on local farms. We've been selling in 20 retailers around New Jersey and get re-orders every week from them. I'd love the opportunity to put a rack of our chips in your store".

Why this pitch works:

- Clearly differentiates himself from the competition
- Proven retail sales demonstrate demand
- Close with what he's looking for from the buyer

Work on your pitch until you're satisfied with it - and that doesn't mean perfection. Get out there and pitch to retailers. Refine it as you get feedback from buyers.

Next, we'll explore how to best tell your story.

Step 2: Tell them your story

Good stories have three elements: A situation, a conflict, and a solution. Similar to paragraphs in writing, stories get told in a certain format. And to be written well, your story doesn't have to be long. But, keep in mind buyers are likely to ask "Why did you start your company?" or "How'd you get into mustard?" Be prepared to answer with a compelling, passionate story. Buyer's are people, too, and they'll get behind you if you have a great story. And be honest. Fabricated stories are the worst.

Step 3: Get into the numbers

Buyers are 'numbers' people. They need to hit a certain margin for your product to work in their store. I've been turned down at stores because my product is too expensive - it wouldn't fit the demographic. This is why store research and having the right numbers is important. Here's what they want to know:

- Your case pack size

- Your price to them (usually delivered)

- The number of skus you have

- Your minimum order

Have this information ready before you walk into the store. They'll be impressed if you already talk shop with them and know buyer lingo.

Step 4: Field their questions

Buyer's questions are hard to anticipate, but take every question one at a time. Don't be disrespectful if they ask a question you've already answered. Buyers have a lot on their mind, so simply repeat the answer and move on. A couple questions you could anticipate answering:

- Do you do demos?
- Are you open to promotions?
- What are your top sellers?
- How can I buy it - through you or distribution?
- How many skus are you looking to get in the store?
- Do stores around us sell it?
- How much is it there?

Step 5: Close by taking action

This is the most important step. Many food business owners meet with buyers without making sure both parties have next steps. Maybe it's a follow up call on Tuesday morning. Maybe it's delivery of an initial order. End with taking action - even on a five minute impromptu meeting. This step is crucial because it shows you're in it to win it -- and not just selling to "another store".

Once you get used to going through the five steps, you'll be a natural. I'd suggest practicing with some family members before you meet with your first buyer. Get your nerves out, breathe, and practice, practice, practice. It's the only way you'll get better with buyer meetings.

Sometimes this 5-step process doesn't work.

Not all buyers are going to jump at your product line. And some pull it in for an initial order and don't re-order it for a number of reasons. Let's explore some of the reasons buyers don't say yes immediately.

Why buyer's don't accept your product line

You might have pitched your heart out. You might have had a delicious product. And you might have a promotional plan to challenge Proctor & Gamble. But, the buyer still doesn't take your product line on.

Here are a couple reasons:

1. There's no room for your product

Shelf space is like real estate. The better the location, the higher price you have to pay to get space there. And some areas of the grocery store are worse than others -- frozen, snacks, and cereal to name a few. In these sections, there might not be any room. I've had to wait as long as 6 months to get on a shelf -- and at that store, I waited 3 years just to get our product considered. Three years!

2. The price isn't right

Your product could be too expensive (it likely won't be too cheap as you're doing small productions). A high price for the wrong demographic is a recipe for disaster. Your product will sit on the shelf, wasting precious shelf space. Solve it by taking a look into where the most ideal locations for your product are - and focus on those buyers.

3. Your category isn't up for review

Some categories only get reviewed once a year. Miss the review period, and you're on the waiting list. To find out when your product's category is reviewed, call or email the buyer. That way, you're not bothering them when they shouldn't be looking at your line.

4. It doesn't look good on the shelf

You want buyers to take your line on without tasting it. You do that through incredibly beautiful packaging. Consumers pick up pretty things. And if it looks too homemade, you may get passed on for another, more established brand.

5. The buyer doesn't like it

Hate to say it, but some buyers won't like your product. It happens to me all the time. Maybe you brought in the wrong samples, or they're the only one making the decision, but it is tough to handle. Not every buyer is going to like your product. Lucky for you, buyer's change jobs quite frequently so it's a good idea to check back in 3 or 6 months.

Don't let a "no" get you down. Follow up, change your packaging, pricing, and test. Find what works best with retail buyers and keep it going.

There might even be a couple questions you don't know how to answer on your first go-around. Here's a list of 10 questions - and how to answer them.

10 Questions retail buyers will ask you (and how to answer them)

Retail stores are one of the best ways to expand your distribution channel and grow your business. They provide for the right location at the right time for your customers to purchase your product. Plus, I've found a lot of people want to buy my products in- store – not online – because it's local to them (and they don't have to buy 6 jars of it to get free shipping).

The downside to having retail as part of your distribution strategy is, it's complex.

There are numbers to deal with, people to call (get over your fear of the telephone), and well, your work isn't done when you fill out the purchase order. You've got to make your product sell so retailers re-order.

Today, I'll tackle one aspect of the retail environment: answering the buyer's questions.

I'm working on getting more retailers in the Boston-area right now – and that means lots of phone call follow-up. Sometimes I get their voicemail (which is another post in it's own right), but other times I actually do get the buyer. And then they ask me interesting questions.

1. What's your story?

Story is everything in food. And you've got to have a compelling one. Did you lose your job and start selling granola? Do you have a family dumpling business? Or maybe you're a young college graduate whose dream is to own an ice cream company. Whatever it is, make your story shine.

How to answer: Keep it short. It's not the most important part of the discussion. Write out five sentences in chronological order. Include a beginning, middle, and end – just like you did in third grade. Simple is better than complex. This is useful when customers ask, too.

2. What makes your product different from everything else on the shelf?

You can't just make another BBQ sauce. There's already 12-16 feet of them in the grocery store. What makes yours different? Put another way: Why should I pull another brand off the

shelf to put you there. To make shelf-space for your products, buyers often have to pull another brand off the shelf. Keep this in mind when you formulate an answer.

How to answer: Many products get differentiated by their health claims: sugar free, gluten free, non-gmo, etc. This may be enough for you to get shelf space, but it also might have to do with your company being local, your amazing food packaging, or unique flavor combinations. Think about this one. It may be the most important on the list.

3. What's your goal?

I just got this one from a buyer. And while thinking on my feet paid off, he was pretty much asking "why would a small Vermont mustard company randomly send a retailer in Boston samples?" When you expand into other states, you'll likely get this question to. But, it tells me retailers want to know why. The buyer said "Do you want to build a brand? Do you want to just sell more mustard?" I answered with this: " I'm on a mission to show New England mustard doesn't have to be bright yellow and it can in fact, be very flavorful. Plus, we do a lot of events in Boston and my customers always ask where they can buy it. I'd like to provide them with an answer." Result: he liked it.

How to answer: Of course you want to say "SELL MORE! SELL MORE!" but that's just not believable. Why did you start your business? And what problem would sending samples solve? Describe the situation, state the problem, and provide a solution. Here's how my answer breaks down:

Situation: We sell at a lot of events in Boston, so we're building a following.
Problem: My loyal Boston fans have no where to buy our mustard.
Solution: Your retail store is a great solution.

That's my why. That's my goal. And why I'm sending you samples. What's your goal?

4. How do you distribute your product?

Buyers ask this to learn how they'll get your product. If it's not easy to order, they won't. It's as simple as that. But, if you're available through four distributors and they use one of them, you're a shoe-in. With that being said, maybe you don't have a distributor. That's fine. Many retailers still buy direct from hundreds of suppliers – and they're happy to add one more.

How to answer: This one is pretty straight-forward. State all your delivery options (direct, distributor, private delivery service, producer coop, etc.). The buyer will likely show interest in one and want to compare prices – direct vs. distributor. More on that in question 10. If you have a minimum order amount, let them know that, too.

 FOODTRUCKEMPIRE

5. Do you do store demos?

You've got to sell product. It simply can't sit there on the shelf or you're going to get swapped out for another brand the buyer believes will move off the shelf better. It's happened to me before, and it's not fun to find out about. Removing a store from our store locations list is like ripping an adhesive bandage off. It hurts. Because buyers are there to help you, they'll often require store demos as a condition to taking your product.

How to answer: YES, YES, YES. You do store demos. Yes, you have time. Yes, you can find someone to do it if you're busy. Demos are crucial to your product's success. Even though I look at them as a necessary evil, you have to do them. Let the buyer know you'll do one a quarter, once a month – whatever. They like to see that you (or your sales team) is involved in helping the retailer sell your product.

6. Where else do you sell your product?

Buyers want to know they won't have a lot of competition – especially for specialty products that may not sell as fast as say, chips or beverages. They also want to know you're committed to making a footprint in the area, which is nice if you already have a couple of retailers in the area. They may say "well, if Joe's Market has your product, I want it to".

How to answer: List area stores out, but state why you came into this store (remember question #3). If you're not in a store near them, pitch the buyer the opportunity they have to be an exclusive (for the time being) retailer in their area. That'll get them excited.

7. Do you have a sell sheet?

Sell sheets are just like magazine advertisements. They're shiny. They have beautiful pictures. And they can get pretty expensive to print. But, they show professionalism. They provide all the info a buyer needs about your product, too.

How to answer: Yes, of course you do. Even if it's made in Microsoft Word, sell sheets are important for buyers because business cards often get lost in the shuffle. (Have you seen a buyer's desk – whoa.)

8. What's your promotional schedule?

What? I have to have promos? Well, they aren't required, but they're definitely encouraged. Retailers like Whole Foods Markets, requires a demo and promotional schedule (at least two times a year). But, think about what a promotion does: No, it doesn't cheapen your product – don't think about it that way. It simply encourages more purchases. And more purchases means you have the opportunity to create more raving fans. And that's never a bad thing.

How to answer: Plan to put your product on promo (with larger retailers) a couple times a year. One of the best times is when you know you'll sell a lot of product. For many condiment

 FOODTRUCKEMPIRE

company's it's the summer. So if you normally move 10 cases a month, maybe you could move 30 if you run a promotion. Before you state your promotions, calculate if you're still going to make money. When you're small, you can't afford to lose money on a promotion.

9. Do you do guaranteed sales?

Back when I owned a small energy bar company, I got this question with every single retailer (and it's one of the reasons I got out of the short-shelf life business). Guaranteed sale (or buy-back) means the buyer has no skin in the game. If your product doesn't sell after a certain time period, you buy it back. Here's an example: you sell 24 muffins at $2.00 – $48 total. You come back next week and find you only sold 3 muffins. That means you buy-back 21 muffins at $2.00 a piece (likely out-of- date or moldy, too). A total of $42.00 – and you can't sell the product to anyone else. You've made $6.00 – which quickly gets eaten up by transportation costs. Guaranteed sale is a nightmare.

How to answer: Well, if you're new to the bakery scene or anything refrigerated, it's smart to do in the beginning when you need to pick up traction with a couple retailers. Ultimately, you never want to do guaranteed sales. It's just not a profitable way to grow your food business.

10. How much does your food product cost?

It almost always comes down to price, it seems. That's because price determines a lot of things: if the retail buyer will buy and if the customer will buy, too. Sometimes, $12 for jam is just too much. But, you've got to know your pricing. Get it memorized. Know if there is flexibility for bulk orders, too.

How to answer: Well, the truth is a good start. Be confident in your pricing. Let them know their unit cost through different distributors and direct. Plus, mentioned the MSRP (manufacturer's suggested retail price). Again, it's suggested. Retailers can mark it up to whatever they want – above or below the MSRP.

Retail is a great way to expand distribution of your food products, but you have to be prepared. Take some time to answer these questions and write them down. If you have a sales team, have a meeting to discuss these. It's important to have everyone on the same page.

In the spirit of keeping things positive, let's assume you landed the new retailer. Now, it's time to make the most of your new relationships. Here's your action plan (also available as a worksheet at the end of the book).

 FOODTRUCKEMPIRE

I Contacted 103 independent retailers. Here are the results (plus what I learned)

One of the first things I learned after running several small food companies was success, albeit defined in many different ways, was dependent on moving a lot of product. This meant I wasn't going to make money moving a mere 30-40 cases a month at my local farmer's market. I needed to move more.

That means selling more!

Sounds obvious, doesn't it? But, it's a lot harder than it looks. I mean, mustard doesn't magically move out of my parent's basement. I have to make it move (quite literally sometimes). I could do more farmer's markets, find some private label accounts, get into more retailers, do more festivals, buy Facebook ads, etc.

For the past 3 months, I've been working on getting into more retail stores. Why? They order relatively frequently and when other revenue streams are dead, I've always got retail. Plus, distribution is king in the food industry.

As the son of an engineer, I'm super analytical and data-driven. I started this project by writing my process down (It helped to have experience in phone sales from my days working for a seller of accounting websites.).

My 5-Step Independent Retailer Process:

1. Acquire a list of retailers (lots of manual work here)
2. Research retailers to determine fit
3. Email to see if they'd like samples (more on what worked later)
4. Send samples
5. Create a follow up schedule and land that account (this was a series of phone calls and emails)

There are sub-processes for the 5 steps as well, but I won't get into those here. With the process down, I started on the first row of my spreadsheet. They didn't want any samples. (Oh, this was going swell). As I worked down the list, I was getting sample requests left and right – mostly over email. Fast forward to the results of my experiment.

The Results:

- Retailers contacted: 103 (by phone and email)

 **FOODTRUCKEMPIRE**

- Samples requested: 34 (33.01% of retailers)
- Orders placed: 10 (9.71% of retailers)
- Revenue: $928.00

It was an interesting experiment. For the countless hours of work I (and ultimately a part-time sales guy) poured into this, I had $928 in sales to show for it — not profit. When I took the costs out, I ended up with about $200 in my pocket. But, it wasn't so much the profit as it was the process.

I think there's more there. This number could be improved.

What I learned:

1. A strict follow-up schedule has to be created (and stuck to)

I lost track of everyone I was talking to. I had no idea who I had been contacted, who got their samples, did they get a phone call or an email. And then days later, they'd fall right back off my radar. To start, I had a phone call/email back-and-forth going on. It worked when I was dealing with a couple retailers, but as the project expanded, it got out of control. I installed Streak CRM in my gmail which helps with the leads pipeline as well as follow-up reminders. The trouble? I'd literally forget to use it. Now, I have a process written down. All that's left is forming a follow up habit.

2. The best email strategy shows customers want to buy your product

I was on my last handful of retailers two weeks ago. I sent out 15 emails and got 10 sample requests back. What worked so well? I used something like "Hey _____, We've heard from a lot of our current customers that _____ would be a great place to carry our _____. Could I send you some samples? Who should I send them to?" I used a couple different variations, but playing the "customer card" worked well, even if it might have been a stretch of the truth. Bottom line: it got my product in the buyer's mouth. Oh, and you have the buyer's name – gold mine!

3. I have to spend my time courting bigger accounts

As you may have seen above, I hired a commissioned sales guy to help me sell into all of these independent retailers. I continue to give him leads on a weekly basis. There are hundreds. He calls/emails and works with me to create a process that works with both of us. When I was sending out 8-10 samples a week, I noticed how much I wasn't doing to build my business. Now, I have a little bit more time to work on large-account sales. Still up to my neck in work (aren't we all), but trying to get dedicated time to work on my business. Not in it. Wish me luck!

4. It can get expensive

Here's what I send every person who requests samples: 3 full-size jars (buyers want to see what the product looks like on the shelf), a sell sheet, a price sheet, a postcard promoting our cookbook, and a handwritten note to the buyer (a simple index card and sharpie – authentic right there!). The jars are individually-wrapped and packing peanuts fill space. Thankfully, the box is free (shout-out to the USPS). All said and done, the sample kit costs me $12 to send (on average). To put that in perspective, the 34 samples I sent out above cost me $408 — almost 50% of my generated sales. But, keep in mind, I'll make my money back on the repeat orders. If you have the sampling budget, it's worth the investment.

5. Never give up

During this time, I attended the Vermont Grocer's Association Annual Meeting (always a fun time catching up with fellow food producers). At the meeting, I listened to a panel on trade-shows and the importance of following up with leads. One of the panelists was Keith, the former owner of Westminster Crackers. He let the crowd know about this follow up technique (which was a folder for every day of the month), but more importantly he stressed the importance of following up until you get a no from the buyer or a "I never want to hear from you again!" And even if you get a "no" it's still not firm. Buyer's change, store's needs change. You never know. I've been working on some of the leads from the big list for months now. I'll get them to order eventually!

Overall, I enjoyed this experiment. I'm going to keep doing it because at the very least it gets my product out there into people's mouths who haven't tried it before.

You're in! How to leverage your new relationship

Getting into a new retailer is only the beginning. You've got to work on the relationship to get the most out of it - whether that's connections to retailers, reorders, or social media partnerships. Here's how to make your relationship a total benefit.

8-Step action plan after you land a new retailer

1. Ship (or deliver) your product on time.

Don't make a crappy first impression. Get your product to the store when you say you'll get it there. Let the buyer (and receiving team) know you're serious about your business.

2. Follow your new retailer on social media

The store is probably on Facebook, Twitter, and Instagram - maybe even Pinterest and LinkedIn. Follow their account so you know when they post new stuff and maybe even mention your product!

3. Post about your new retailer on social media

This is quite obvious, but let your following know about your new retailer! I like to build up a list of new retailers and then do one big post. That way, I don't get a ton of "new store!" posts on my newsfeed. And add a picture if you can - that makes it easier to be shared and lends a little bit of personality.

4. Add your new store to a store locator (or your own list)

Store locators help your customers find local retailers to purchase your product when you're not at the farmer's market or an annual festival. Plus, you get a cool map that shows your progress. One tip -- don't list your distributors and ask customers to call them - they don't need to explain where customers can find your product. Ask them to contact you if you don't have a store locator.

5. Send a couple units to the store for employees and managers

This helped me build up a following in my most popular retailers. When I get a new retailer on board, I leave samples with the buyer or send them with the first order to go into the employee break room. And when I do demos, I purposefully go after the employees who walk by as they are in direct contact with the customer. You want them to recommend your product.

6. Schedule your first demo within 2 weeks (if possible)

Get your demo on the calendar. Some stores have you schedule multiple weeks ahead of time. For example, Whole Foods is typically 10 days -- other stores are longer. Ask for the demo coordinator's contact information and have some dates in mind for your first demo. Why demo so soon? You want your product to move off the shelf almost immediately so you can show your buyer that your product is moving well and customers love it.

7. Create a follow-up schedule post-sale

This is where many small food producers fall short. They get a new retail account and move on to the next one. You have to follow up. And one way to do it is to create a follow up schedule. Here's my example: I have nearly 50 direct accounts, a couple distributors, and then my distributor's accounts. I simply schedule a time every month (it's recurring in my Google Calendar) and email all of my direct accounts. Some move product quicker than others, so I'll send a note or call when I feel they may be running low on product.

8. Run Facebook advertising within a 10-mile radius of the location (optional)

Step 8 is optional because it can get expensive, although Facebook does allow you to set your daily spend limit. Why I use Facebook ads: When I have a retailer who is far away from Vermont, a demo gets expensive. So expensive, to where the profits from my initial sales are wiped out. So, I invest a couple bucks in Facebook advertising within a 10-mile radius of the store and ship samples to do a passive demo (when no one is standing at the demo table). Later in this guide, you'll learn more ways to use Facebook advertising to grow your business.

Make this action plan a habit whenever you land a new retail account. That way it'll happen almost automatically and your retail buyers will appreciate the added support. Now, it's time to get your product there. You could drive it to the store, but there are a couple other alternatives. Let's explore those next.

5 Hacks to get your product to the shelf

Use a Local Delivery Service to Distribute Your Food Product

Remember when you drove all the way across the state to your newest retailer? It was great the first time, but restocking the shelf with your second order was a lot of gas and time. That's where local delivery companies come in hand. For just a couple bucks, they'll likely pick up and deliver your product for you - and you don't have to go anywhere. In Vermont, there are several companies who do this. It's $15 for up to 50 pounds - and for us, that's a normal order. Beats driving two hours for one delivery!

Increase Your minimum order

During Green Mountain Mustard's first two years in business, we had no minimum order... just to grow. Now, we are smarter and have a minimum order – it's two cases (24 units) - not too big, but it makes sure we're moving volume - the key to any food business. If you travel across town just for a purchase order of 6 jars and you're going to lose money. With a minimum order, you're able to make money with each delivery.

Consolidate deliveries on certain days of the week

Doing deliveries every day throws off your schedule. That's why you should consolidate your deliveries on certain days of the week. Maybe one county is Mondays and the next county over gets deliveries on Fridays. That leaves the middle of the week for producing product, doing office admin work, and calling on new retailers. Why don't you consider drawing a route out that helps you get all your deliveries done faster?

 FOODTRUCKEMPIRE

Learn how to sell food online

Back when I owned an energy bar company, I delivered to 20 different stores every week. It took a ton of time and not making much money. Green Mountain Mustard has both direct-accounts food distributors. But, food distribution eats into your gross margin. Food websites are growing and there are popular easy to use ecommerce platforms like Storenvy, Shopify and Etsy all focused on small artisanal businesses.

Partner with another food producer

You probably know at least a dozen other small food producers just like yourself... all delivering to the same stores, right? Consolidate deliveries with each other... such as "everyone delivers to a certain store on Mondays". If you start doing this more often with the same stores, you may want to look at working with a food distributor (covered in the next section).

What I learned from meeting with 3 big (and one small) buyers

I get nervous when I meet with buyers.

It doesn't matter the size. One or 100, I get a pit in my stomach. And over the last few weeks, I've met with buyers who have the power to launch my business into the stratosphere. We talked about all kinds of things. Product line, top-sellers, pricing, promotions — you name it.

I learned a boatload.

And I'm passing on the lessons (and the huge list of vocabulary) on to you.

Here goes!

Meeting #1: Large distributor in Texas Promotions move more product

This was my first time experiencing an intro promotion. Not only did I have to meet a lowered shelf-price, but for the first four weeks I had to do an intro deal that took a $1 off our shelf-price. I just have to get used to these promotions. I know it will move more product. Plus, it may even get us on end-caps which means lots of product to be ordered. Coupled with a promotion, it's sure to move. I've experimented with promotions locally in Vermont, but nothing on a larger scale. My mindset when we talk promos? Let's play ball. It's all about negotiation and what works for you: the manufacturer, the distributor, and the retailer.

 FOODTRUCKEMPIRE

Freight means an increased shelf-price

It's expensive to ship anything in the US. Anything. And if you ship glass jars like me, you know what I'm talking about. This particular distributor was aiming for a specific price on the shelf and requested I come down in price to help offset freight costs. I justified it because she's likely to order several pallets of product. But, it also further emphasizes the importance of getting your product cost down as low as you can. I'm still struggling with that, but working on it!

Christmas is in July

I've been thinking about the holidays since March – scheduling shows and festivals. And retailers?

They're right on my tail. July is holiday time at a lot of large retailers. That means be ready with holiday-themed product launches and samples. Holiday decisions have already been made for this particular distributor and another one (not in this list) has already discussed their holiday strategy. I'll keep this in mind for products I'm launching for summer next year.

Meeting #2: Large distributor in New York It's all in the details

I just got a follow up call last week from this distributor and we hammered through numbers: minimum order quantity, hi x ti (pronounced high-tie — more on that in an upcoming vocabulary lesson), terms, cases per pallet, and more. When dealing with larger distributors and larger customers, these details matter. You're not selling to independents anymore, Dorothy! It's no longer – this is fantastic mustard, can I grab 4 cases? It's intense number crunching, down to the last penny.

I made sure to let the distributor know that I was flexible on all the numbers I gave her. I did this to help win the deal and move more product. If there's one thing I've learned in the 4 years doing this, it's that flexibility goes a long way — and ultimately leads to increased sales.

Be strategic about the large retailers you choose

We're a super-premium product. Easily 3 - 5x more expensive than what is currently on the shelf. That means we've got to be strategic about where we put our product. Where is it going to move well? Are there required promotions?

This distributor presented two large clients she works with and highly recommended we go with one over the other strictly because of volume. She said we'd move double, if not triple, the other major chain. It made me realize I can't just throw darts at a board and hope my product gets picked up. I have to strategically target where I want to see my product. And focus all of my effort on landing those deals.

 FOODTRUCKEMPIRE

Demo support is going to cost some money

This particular distributor is working to pitch our mustard to a regional retailer. It's awesome to think about, but what does the demo support look like? How do you demo in 100+ stores? At $75-100 a demo, 100 demos is going to run you $10,000. Then you've got to do it again in 2 months. It adds up.

That's why one of my priorities for the next few months is to come up with a demo system that can be replicated in different parts of the area through hired help. Our local demo guy in Vermont who does a demo or two a week is willing to be my guinea pig on how to best demo your food product. I'll keep you posted.

Meeting #3: Large distributor in Canada

Exclusivity is the name of the game

Many distributors and importers request exclusivity for the entire country. The whole thing. Border to border. Why? Because they need to know they're going to be the only one selling it, you haven't undercut them, or "so-and-so just pitched that to me last week". It makes the importer's job practically useless. After doing some research, many importers and foreign distributors have exclusivity in their contracts. Come to think of it, it's how the beverage industry works in Vermont — you can only have one distributor for your alcoholic beverages. I'm not worried too much about the exclusivity. In fact, it's a lot easier to deal with one account manager for the entire country than say 10 or 20 who are targeting the same customers.

Be ready to print new labels

Wow. The health and label regulations for different countries are fascinating. While I understand we need to have French/English translation on our labels, we also need to have "prepared mustard" on our labels. This is enough to know I'm going to need separate labels for Canadian distribution (of which I have a disproportionate demand for now...). This costs money, obviously, but it seems like I should be limiting the countries I work with to export. I'm currently working with 3 importing companies across the globe. That may mean new labels for three countries. We'll see...

The idea of an "export" price

When talking pricing with my exporter, he mentioned an "export price". This is a price that's below distributor pricing that accounts for the duties, taxes, tariffs and other fun stuff importers experience when bringing in product. While I haven't gone forward with this, it's worth exploring. Also keep in mind that importers typically order in pallet quantities, so it makes sense to give them a break.

Meeting #4: My home-town grocery store buyer

Work with your buyer – not against them

For 4 years, I delivered mustard to this store when they were out. There wasn't a buyer. No one ordered anything. I dropped it off to an upset grocery manager who wasn't expecting our products. "Well, you have three sold out skus. Don't you want to fill the space?" She responded – "Maybe not". It was then I knew changes were brewing.

After being read the riot act about "how things worked now", I made sure to create rapport with the buyer quickly. "I'm not here to argue with you. I'm here to work with you. If that means I need to transfer you to my distributor, then that works — just let me know". After that, things went well. Bottom line is that communication between all parties involved is essential.

Harsh reality: You will lose facings

I've never had to fight to keep facings in a store before. I've always just added new flavors as I saw fit. After all, it was my home-town store. Not anymore. The grocery manager was reviewing the 8' condiment section. Lots of companies wanted their products on the shelf — and I wanted to stay on. I jockeyed to at least fill the facings that were sold-out and to keep 4 skus – our most popular flavors. I figured if locals wanted other flavors they could pick them up from us. Grocery stores are consolidating. Corporations are acquiring small companies like yours and mine – just for more shelf space. It's time to get the gloves on.

Do deliveries in the early morning hours

The last direct delivery I made was at 5:57am. Receiving opened at 5:00am. The big trucks from UNFI were already backed up to the loading docks. The receiver was friendly and had me on my merry way in minutes.

Compare this to delivering just shy of 3:00pm – near the end of the receiver's day. They hate you. They shouldn't, but they do. Receivers deal with the most problems – more than anyone else in the store – because they are in charge of the movement (and sometimes the ordering) of product to get on the shelf.

Oh, and did I mention lifting heavy things. I would never want that job. That's why I'm going to make my deliveries in the morning when the receiver still has a smile on his/her face.

5 Keys to retail success for your food business

After several years of selling Green Mountain Mustard at various farmer's markets I decided to launch this little venture in grocery retail stores. The result is now we can be found in over 70

stores across the Northeast and other states. So I wanted to give other food entrepreneurs advice on Getting on the Shelf and most importantly, staying on the shelf!

There are no secrets to this success and like most of you, I learned the hard way, so here are my 5 keys to success and feel free to let me know how these work out for you in getting on the shelf so you can get on the consumers plate!

You've got to get on the shelf and stay there

It takes a lot of work - mainly maintenance of relationships. Sure, it's easy to get into more retailers, but what about keeping your shelf-space? That's the most important key to success.

If your product isn't moving, it won't be reordered. It's as simple as that. How do you make sure your product is top of the list for a purchase order? Take a look at these five tips to make retail a success marketing channel for your food products.

Don't expect food brokers and distributors to sell for you

When I landed my first distributor. I thought I was golden. I thought I'd be in hundreds of stores in just a few months. Unfortunately, that wasn't the case. Distributors and brokers represent thousands of products.

They can't possibly single your product out. That means you've got to be the one pounding the pavement - going into stores to drop samples off and talk to store managers. Use your distributor as a way to distribute your product. Makes sense, right?

Follow up with grocery and supermarket buyers

Simply dropping off samples and saying a prayer isn't going to get your products on the shelf at the busiest grocery store in town. You have to follow up... let's say once per quarter. Yes, even if it seems like it's annoying. The buyer forgets about you the second your samples leave your hands. After a couple days, follow up with them by email or phone. Follow up is also necessary once you get on the shelf. Call your buyer to see how things are going. Spend your time developing ideas to present effective in store trade promotions to the buyer during your follow up calls and meetings.

Do monthly in store demos

Demos are awesome. They get you in-front of new customers, and you meet loyal fans (who then give you ways to use your product). Plus, you gain brownie points from your buyer for spending an afternoon dishing out samples.

This shows your commitment to the retailer and your desire to push more product. Many stores only allow one demo slot per month. Take advantage of that and schedule your next demo after you finished your last one.

Clean up and keep an eye on your shelf space

No one likes dusty jars - even if they just made it onto the shelf. Dusty jars tells consumers your product is old, close to expiration, and it's not popular. Shine your jar tops with a microfiber cloth, straighten your facings, and pull product forward. This attention to detail helps you sell more products.

Plus, going into retailers lets you know if you need to deliver more product. That means, you'll have clean shelves and fully-stocked product. A perfect mix for increased sales of your food products.

Start small & grow

A lot of food companies want to grow at lightning speed from the beginning. I urge you to take it slower. Why? Because you'll be much more organized. You'll have processes figured out and you'll know what works in retail. Going from 5 stores to 500 takes time, money, systems, maintenance, and a lot of sweat. Start small, figure everything out, and then make your move to shelf stardom.

Retail isn't meant to be a frustrating sales channel. It just takes a lot of time to build up your store count and get product moving. With these tips, you'll get a great retail program in place.

Best of luck dominating the store shelves!

I want to end with an inspiring story from Anne, a reader from Oregon. Anne and I started emailing back and forth in January 2014. Her first email included this story:

"My husband and I have been trying to start a health food business for 3 years. We started out delivering produce by bicycle and failed miserably. We created a multi- farm CSA that coordinated multiple organic farms and delivered weekly boxes by bicycle. We were using a licensed commercial kitchen for our distribution point and that got us interested in food processing. We started baking organic bread (while continuing our produce delivery) and we bought ingredients, packaging, displays, etc for literally hundreds of different products from sourdough bread to custom cakes to pizza to raw vegan desserts and snacks.

After losing $13,000 of our own savings, we were broke, homeless, and living in a tent with 2 young kids and one more on the way (October 2014).

Our products were amazing but it seems that making outstanding tasting healthy foods was all we were good at. We gave away so much product and made horrible business decisions. **We**

knew nothing of how to run a business. So we ended it all but held onto one small part: Raw vegan kale chips.

We began making only kale chips literally with only a couple hundred dollars in November 2014 and quickly paid off all of our farmers from the produce delivery fiasco. We started selling at the local farmers market and to 3 stores locally."

This story is inspiring. It shows how anyone can get started in the food business with however little they have. Even after losing thousands, Anne and her family were determined to bring their kale chips to market.

No matter the challenges you face, you can build a business - and a successful one! As you hit bumps in the road, remember why you started. Look back at all the lives you've positively affected through your food.

That's why you're in this business. **To bring love to the table.**

Part 3:

The Ultimate Guide to Profitable Co-Packing

Congratulations! You've made it to part 3 of this book… The ultimate guide to profitable co-packing! This guide will help determine if co-packing is right for your company, how to find the right co-packer, and how to build a better relationship.

Let's jump in! Navigating the world of co-packing is…

- Intimidating

- Confusing

- Frustrating

- Risky

- Rewarding

- Expensive

And more. It's not for the faint of heart. Even though you're having someone else make your product, you're still involved in the management of your business. In other words, the weight of food manufacturing isn't completely off your shoulders.

After reading this guide, you'll have a better idea if you want to take on a co-packer. But first, you've got to answer some tough questions.

Before you head down the co-packing route, there's a couple of things you have to sort out with yourself and your business partners.

Don't brush this step off.

These are the tough questions. The questions no one wants to talk about. The questions you have to work through before you even start your search.

Just like starting up your food business and answering questions like "Where am I going to get the money?" and "Do I want to do this?", getting started with co-packing has its own set of questions. Let's explore a few of them:

5 questions to answer before you look for a co-packer:

1. Do I want to give up control of making my product?

Spend some time with this one. It's the most important question, because it fundamentally impacts your business. Do you want to give up control of your manufacturing? For many food producers, they want to be the only one who makes their product. Maybe it comes out better, maybe it's cheaper, or maybe you're a control freak.

Ok, I'm kidding about that last one. Regardless, let's look at pros and cons of outsourcing your manufacturing:

Pros:

May be cheaper: Often, outsourcing your manufacturing is cheaper because you don't have the overhead of your own kitchen and you can make a lot more product for the same amount of money.

More time for sales: Sales drives your food company's growth. So, wouldn't it be great if you had more time to sell your food product? Of course! Outsource your manufacturing and you've got your wish: more time to find new retailers, do store demos, and attend local fairs and festivals.

Less to worry about: Sure, you've got to manage the manufacturing process, but taking the manufacturing off your plate means you have less to worry about. Co-packers worry about equipment breaking, when they're going to schedule you, and the ingredients you have.

Cons

May be expensive: As you'll learn later in the guide, co-packing can be expensive. There's high day rates, storage fees and more that make up the co-packing industry.

Quality control: If you copack out of state, quality control is out of your hands. If something goes wrong, your co-packer has to worry about it. You can't do much. This is also true with quality control. Generally, only when you pick up your product do you notice quality issues. That's risky.

Lots of inventory: When someone else is making your product, you might need to make more product to get your costs down. More product means more cash is tied up in product inventory. And more cash tied up? We all know that may spell doom if you can't seem to move your product fast enough.

It's a tough decision to give up manufacturing your food product, but that's what co-packing is. Let's move on to the next question you need to ask yourself.

2. Do I have the cash to co-pack?

Reader Beware: Co-packing can quickly empty your bank account. Let's say you have 10 recipes. At upwards of $600 - $800 per day, a co-packer is likely to run 23 flavors per day. That means 5 days of co-packing. Which really means $3,000 - $4,000. And that's just for your co-packer. Include ingredients and packaging, you're likely to be out $10,000 just for a couple days of manufacturing. See how everything can quickly add up?

Cash is king in any business. And making sure you have enough of it is key to growing your business.

When you're producing in your house, everything is cheap. You have no kitchen rental time to worry about (since you have 24/7 access), you have no employees to pay, and ingredient storage is practically free.

When you switch to co-packing, your company has to pay for all of this and then some. There are tons of costs associated with co-packing that you don't incur at home. Do you have the cash to make the transition?

Whether the money comes from your current cash reserves, bank loans, credit cards, or friends/family is up to you. Make sure you have some money because if you're going along and all of sudden there's no cash then you have no company. And no company means your products are coming off the shelf.

3. How will you manage everything?

How are you going to oversee quality issues? Who is going to interact with the kitchen manager? Make sure you've got a team member or members to manage everything.

Who is going to make sure you've got enough ingredients? Who is going to make sure you've got recipes and production setup? While many of these responsibilities are part of the copackers, you're going to want to have a point person to manage everything.

If you're the sole owner of your food biz, you'll manage everything (surprise, surprise). Make sure you've got processes and systems in place (plus software to run your food business). You'll be glad to have the system in place before everything goes awry.

4. Is there a co-packer in your area?

Doing an initial co-packer search may yield no results. But, thinking outside your area. Maybe your co-packer is in the next state over. I know many manufacturers who co-pack in Vermont, but they run their companies from all over the place. Kansas, Massachusetts, and New York City for example. But I also know Vermont companies who co-pack out of state because there is a co-packer who better meets their company's needs.

Don't like driving 10 hours to produce your product? Yeah...I don't blame you. Both of my co-packers have never been more than an hour away. But, you may not have any co-packers in your location.

Before you give up because you think there aren't any co-packers in your area, try asking around. Talk with other food producers to see what they do. And who knows maybe you'll build a shared kitchen (and that's a whole other guide in its own right!).

5. Why do you want to do this?

The final question is more of a personal, introspective question: *Why* do you want to have your products co-packed? A lot of business owners I've spoken to over the past few years have done it to save tons of time. But, don't just make that your reason.

Think about it. It's important to nail this down. Don't do it because everyone else is doing it.

- Do it because it saves you time
- Do it because it saves you money
- Do it because you get more resources
- Do it because you'll meet industry veterans
- Do it because you want to

And most importantly, do it because it's the right move for your company. After figuring out the outsourcing manufacturing question, this is the second most important question. It can shape your company's future and influence decisions to grow your company.

And remember....

All of these questions should be discussed with anyone who has a major role in your company: business partners, family, friends, business advisors, and even small business consultants (if you use one). You never know when someone is going to suggest something or connect you with someone you didn't know beforehand.

Get these questions answered. But them in a word document, write them in your notebook, or just talk about everything face to face.

The next section is about why you would even need to consider using a co-packer. And many of the ideas have to do with running your business for not emotionally driven reasons.

Let's continue...

 FOODTRUCKEMPIRE

Why would you ever need a co-packer?

You may be wondering why so many food companies co-pack their products. It turns out, there's a lot of business driven reasons to copack.

Why does everything have to be a business decision?

Yes. You make a food product. Yes, you're passionate about it, and yes, it tastes great. But when it comes down to it, you own a light manufacturing company. A company operates around the clock. Problems arise and decisions have to be made.

How you react to problems and opportunities is part of business.

And co-packing is one of those decisions. It's a business decision. Are you going to save money? Are you going to meet demand? You be the judge of that. Here are a couple reasons companies have decided to move from their home or shared kitchen to co-packing:

1. Demand is just too big for your home kitchen

If you can start out in your home kitchen, start there. It's easy to get off the ground. You have low overhead (since you own your house). Plus, consumers are loving the handcrafted, smallbatch movement. Only when you make something in your house can you call it "homemade".

But sometimes, **consumer demand goes beyond your stove top** and out of your single oven.

First of all, congrats! It's a big move to get out of the house. I've done it with one of three companies. It's scary, fun, exhilarating, and absolutely terrifying at the same time. Plus, growing a food business is tough when you're competing with over 120,000 other products in the grocery store. This is a huge milestone. Congratulations!

Ok, let's get serious...

What does that mean for your little food biz?

You need to produce in larger quantities. And that means leaving the kitchen you've called home for the past year or two. That means you've got to look at other options in your area. One of those options is co-packing. As you work through this guide you'll learn if co-packing is the right decision for you.

2. You need to abide by state laws

Not everyone has the luxury of starting their food business from their home kitchen. Only 14 states have the right to preheat their stoves. And even then, they may only be able to produce

baked goods, not a processed food like mustard, BBQ sauce, or marinades. Consider yourself lucky.

What laws are there to abide by?

- FDA inspected facility
- Food Safety Modernization Act
- USDA Laws & Regulations (only if you handle raw meat products)
- ThirdParty Audit Certification (needed if you want to sell to Whole Foods)

And that's just a short list. These laws force people to manufacture outside their home. It dramatically increases startup costs, but it's the same reason many states lack smallbatch goodies it's simply too expensive to start. I know, it's unfortunate many Americans haven't experienced the creativity of small food companies.

If you're in a state where home bakeries and processing isn't permitted, look into leasing commercial kitchen space to get started. You should only look at co-packing when you have the demand to sustain it (see #1).

3. You'd rather sell your product

Let's face it. Being stuck in a kitchen leaning over a 190 degree kettle isn't glamorous. You smell like your product, machines break, and you never get around to doing anything else. That means limited selling, networking, and business development. **If you have limited time to sell, you have limited time to build your business.**

It's a harsh reality of the food industry. Many small food producers are stuck making their product and don't have time to sell it and build a business. Sure, you could outsource the sales function, but nobody sells your product better than you do.

That's why co-packing is a smart move.

Co-packing gives you the flexibility to be the sales person you want to be. Want to build a hot sauce empire? You've got the time now. Want to be represented by distributors across the country? You've got the time.

Remember, the only way you'll stay in business is if you can move enough cases of your products to be profitable. And to do that, you may need to let other people manage certain parts of your business.

Plus, moving more product means you're growing your business. And that means you can quit that pesky full time job of yours. Oh, and speaking of jobs...

FOODTRUCKEMPIRE

4. You work fulltime and need someone else to make the product

Working 50 - 60 hours a week on top of slaving over a stove to make jam is not an ideal work life balance. Things can get crazy pretty fast long nights, equipment breaking, you know the deal.

Many of you need to have another income to support your dream of running a food business.

Just like you, I worked full time while growing my company. Yes, it inhibited growth for a few years, but I needed to support myself. As I grew my company, the afterwork hours weren't enough to meet demand.

I needed a change.

That's when I turned to co-packing. If I could have someone else make my product with my oversight, I could devote my afterwork and weekends hours to building a business. You can do the same thing!

If you're exhausted from working full time, plus running a part time food business, think about co-packing. Trust me, the first run will totally be worth it.

Think about it: no more chopping produce, no more smelling like your product for days, and my personal favorite no more capping. That's what you pay someone else to do. Assuming you have the money to pay for a co-packer (which is more likely if you have a fulltime job), it's worth it's weight in gold to build your dream while someone else manufactures your product.

Once you establish a relationship with your co-packer, and you're ready to leave your full time job, you'll have TONS of time for sales, meeting with new retailers, doing store demos, etc. This is the ideal situation. That is, of course, if you like sales and marketing! If you don't, keep making your product and hire an outside sales team. But, that's a whole other book in its own right!

5. You can't find your own kitchen space.

Finding kitchen space is flatout hard. No one has to tell you that. Some companies search for kitchen space for years. Whether you're looking for the perfect copacker, a shared kitchen to help you grow, or a restaurant kitchen to rent, you may never find kitchen space.

And not to mention the possibility of your own kitchen space that's just plain expensive, time consuming, and from other producers I've talked to, quite the nightmare.

What this comes down to is you need a place to make your product.

 FOODTRUCKEMPIRE

You can't go too long without producing, right?. This means you need to find a kitchen to quickly meet demand. That really means co-packing is one of the best solutions. Here's a couple reasons why:

1. If you have recipes ready, co-packers can ramp up quickly

2. You can often produce what you need, when you need it

3. It may, financially, be a better move for your company (no multi year lease to deal with)

4. Buying equipment to better fit your copacker is better than buying the *whole* kitchen.

5. (I'll reiterate this one) You have time for sales!

Kitchen searching requires you to be flexible.

If you're looking for a kitchen and things aren't panning out, look at your requirements. Maybe you don't need that much storage space. Maybe you don't need an enormous bottling line.

You may have to sacrifice a few things to find the perfect kitchen. But always keep a co-packer in mind when something's just not working for you.

What it comes down to is this:

You need to find the manufacturing solution that works best for you and your company.

If that's produced by yourself, keep doing that. If that's choosing to have someone else produce for you that works, too. Take time to weigh your options. Talk to friends, family, other food producers, business advisors, etc. Get everyone's opinion. But remember, it's ultimately your decision.

There is no right or wrong decision here. Only what's right for you!

The rest of this ebook assumes you've taken the plunge to search for and work with a co-packer to produce your product. Even if you'd still like to produce in your own kitchen, I urge you to read the rest of the guide. It may shed light on some problems you've been having in your own production or spark ideas to adapt for your own business.

Let's press on!

So you've made the decision to get your product co-packed.

Pop open a bottle of awesome champagne! Seriously, though, it's a big decision. Congrats! It also means your company is growing. Typically, companies choose co-packing when demand for their product increases to a point they can't handle it anymore.

Let's get right to it then, shall we?

There's a lot to know about co-packing your product. It's nothing short of a complicated process. There are many moving parts. To break it down, I wrote this guide in sections.

Here's just a few things you'll learn:

- How to find a co-packer in your area
- Selecting the right co-packer for you
- How much it costs to work with a co-packer (plus hidden cost they don't tell you about)
- The top three secrets to a good co-packing relationship
- How to have the co-packer go beyond just making your product
- What happens if you need to switch co-packers?

It's a *ton* of information. And it's organized as best as possible to make it not only easy for you to digest, but you'll even learn something, too. Wherever possible, there are actionable steps for you to build out your co-packing plan so that you're not meeting with co-packers without knowing anything (plus, that's super embarrassing).

How the guide is structured:

- Summaries Cliff notes just for you.
- Lists and bullets
- Easy, quick, digestible points so you don't have to read every word.
- Real Life stories for my own adventures

You can also download worksheets and an updated companion I wrote for this book called 25 Epic Mistakes I've Made in My Food Business. You can download all of this for free here: https://foodtruckempire.com/fbk-join/.

Now that I've covered the structure of the guide, it's time to get to the meat of this guide: how to select and work with a co-packer to bring your company's products to the next level. First up is the question I get most often: **How do I find a co-packer?** Let's explore your options.

How to Find a co-packer

This is the step that takes the longest amount of time. You can't work with just any co-packer. They have to have the right equipment, be priced right, and you have to actually like the people who make your product. Sounds stupid, but believe me, being friends with your copacker pays

in spades when you're in a jam.

The search to find the perfect co-packer is a long, detailed process. It's near impossible to even *know* the companies that co-pack in your area. Sure, you could do a quick Google search, but oftentimes co-packing companies are hiding in the weeds (plus, they're not exactly pros at search engine optimization).

That's why I've got a few ideas to help you find your copacker.

Three ways to find a co-packer in your area:

As I said above, finding a co-packer isn't as simple as a Google search. The two co-packers I've used have both been found by word of mouth. Yes it still works! Here are a couple avenues you can take to start making a list.

1. Ask other food producers

This is how I found my co-packers. I simply struck up a conversation with other food producers, either at events or farmer's markets. It's not like it's a secret or anything. Food producers will tell you where their product is made. After all, it gets them in good graces with their kitchen manager.

But, there's a right way to approach this. Don't just walk up to a producer and ask "Where is your product made?" that's like walking up to a girl in the bar and kissing her before saying hello (Ok, maybe not, but you get the idea).

Engage in conversation. Ask them about their process, when they started, their favorite flavor, what they've learned in the industry. Get to know them for a little bit. Then, when you feel you have a certain level of trust, ask about referrals (not only about co-packing, but ingredient suppliers, packaging suppliers, etc).

This helps the other producer feel comfortable. Plus, they may actually produce in their own kitchen. And, they may not have considered co-packing for other people as another revenue source. It's not ideal because it takes away from their time to market their company, but it could be an avenue to larger equipment to meet demand and then phase over to co-packing product.

If they do use a co-packer, you're in luck!

Many food producers speak highly of their co-packer and happy to refer you. Why would they do that? They might get a referral bonus! With my second copacker, the hot sauce vendor who referred me got a couple free cleanings (Yep he makes the kitchen quite messy).

How to make the co-pack referral work for you:

1. Ask for their company information (or just take a business card)

2. Ask for the co-packers information

3. Get a general idea of how they operate. That way, you already have questions.

4. Follow up that day or the following day post three sticky notes if you have to Don't forget! 5. Follow up again if you don't hear back within 35 business days. (Yes, seriously)

Further in the guide, you'll learn how to handle the first copacker meeting and what questions to ask. For now, we're still trying to find you a co-packer. Let's make that job one (or, if you want to, speed ahead to the section about visiting co-packers for the first time).

Let's explore the next way to find a co-packer: industry websites.

2. Look on food industry websites

There are numerous industry websites to find a co-packer (and learn a TON about running and growing your food business). Here are links to industry sites with multiple conversations on finding a co-packer.

- SmallFoodBiz.com
- Recipal.com
- FoodStarter.com
- SpecialtyFoodResource.com
- FoodTruckEmpire.com

These may not be in your location, but many of these sites have forums you can post on to find a co-packer closer to you. Regardless, bookmark these sites so you can refer back to them. They provide a great avenue for you to meet other food producers and ask questions about starting, running, and growing your business.

3. Contact your state agriculture department

You'll notice a couple of those links above are links to state agriculture departments that have specific food processing programs. These are goldmines of information. The team of employees at the state level know almost everything there is to know about the food business including finding a co-packer. They'll be glad to help you out.

Here are a few links to the most popular state agriculture departments:

- Vermont - https://tax.vermont.gov/business-and-corp/industry-guidance/agriculture
- New York - https://agriculture.ny.gov/

 FOODTRUCKEMPIRE

- California - https://www.cdfa.ca.gov/
- Nebraska - https://nda.nebraska.gov/
- New Hampshire - https://www.agriculture.nh.gov/
- Massachusetts -
  https://www.mass.gov/info-details/massachusetts-department-of-agriculture-divisions

Ask for the person who works with small food producers. They'll know exactly what you're going through and give you the resources to build your food business not just help you find a co-packer.

What if you can't find your department of agriculture or they're low on available resources?

Your next best bet is to work with the small business administration.

There are local chapters all over the place, plus the counseling is 100% free. Here's a list of all the small business development centers in the nation.Get in touch with your local chapter. They'll get you set up with an advisor.

Why work with an SBDC advisor?

They know the landscape. They've likely worked with other food producers facing the same problems, and they have a network that extends far beyond just family and friends. If they don't know where you can find a co-packer, chances are they have a client who can.
Bottom line: take advantage of state agencies. It's free like zero dollars. They offer tons of resources, free advice, and someone to talk things through with.

As you navigate the crazy world of co-packing, it's nice to have someone to listen to your challenges and help you make a decision. Plus, the SBDC folks are good with numbers, so they'll make sure you're making money, too. Always a plus.

After all of this talking with state agencies and figuring out where other food producers make their product, you may not end up with a co-packer to make your product.

What happens if you can't find a co-packing space?

Take a deep breathe. Maybe you found a co-packer but they're not ready for you or don't have the space in their production schedule. This is often the case with co-packers who have anchor tenants (large food producers who pay to keep the space open rent, lights, etc. But, that's because they're there a lot producing their products. They are supported by a bunch of small producers (like you) who take up the remaining time the kitchen sits idle.

Whatever the reason, if you can't find a co-packer in your hometown it's not the end of the world. There simply might not be space in your area. It's also entirely possible co-packers are at their max in regards to the number of products they can produce. And getting a bigger facility doesn't exactly happen overnight.

So, where does that leave you?

You could start your own co-packing kitchen, but then you'd be a co-packer not a food producer. My current copacker is balancing time between making other products (like mine) and finding the time to keep shelves stocked with her own product line, too. It's a delicate balance I'm sure you don't want to get into.

Opening your own facility is off the table. What's next?

Turns out you might have to get creative. There are tons of options to make large batches of product to meet demand. While not the subject of this guide, let's quickly look at a couple of them:

1. Church kitchen

Depending on what you're producing, church kitchens are a great place to make larger quantities of product. There won't be a filler or labeling machine, but you get access to a state certified commercial kitchen.

2. High school (or any school) cafeteria

I've been in my fair share of school cafeterias and they rival any other kitchen establishment I've seen. Just like churches, the equipment is limited. Plus, you may not be able to produce certain products because of allergies. But, you may be able to get in here for free. It's worth a shot.

3. Restaurant (after hours)

I know several food producers who produce after local restaurants have closed their doors. It's called the graveyard shift.

While it's obviously not ideal, some food producers love to make their product so much that they'll make it in the wee hours of the morning before the restaurant opens for breakfast. Have you thought about asking a local restaurant to use their kitchen? Nothing ventured, nothing gained.

4.Shared Kitchen

Is there a shared kitchen in your area where multiple producers share the space? There are several here in Vermont and throughout the northeast. They may be a great stepping stone for

your business while you reach a certain volume with your product. See the tips above regarding asking producers about a co-packer to find a shared kitchen in your town (or at least close by.)

Selecting the right co-packer for your food business

If you're lucky, you've got several copackers to choose from. If not, you'll have to make your copacker work until you can find another facility or open your own. If you have the luxury of choosing, read on.

Finding the best co-packer for the job is tough.

There's so many factors at play: space, time, money, capabilities, current kitchen tenants etc. Everything should influence your decision. Why? Because when and if you have to switch co-packers, it costs a lot of money and time to move everything over.

This section helps you make the right decision the first time.

Below, you'll find a list of things to consider as you tour different kitchens, meet kitchen managers, talk with current producers, and assess the company. This is by no means an exhaustive list, but gives you a great starting point.

12 Things to consider when selecting a co-packer

1. Size of the facility

How big is the kitchen? Is there enough room for you to produce? And don't forget: take into account any space you'll need should you have to bring in a specific piece of equipment to produce your product. I've produced in 700 square foot kitchens and 7,000 square foot kitchens. Both have met my needs, but the smaller space has met my needs better.

Think storage space, too.

You've got to keep everything stored there (or truck it in and out for each production). And by everything, I mean raw materials/ingredients, all of your packaging (glass jars, plastic caps, labels, boxes, hang tags, etc), and if you ship out of the facility, your finished goods will also need a pallet to stay on.

You're not the only producer.

There may be a number of producers who already lay claim to much of the space. The question you (and the production manager) have to answer is, "is there enough room for your company to move in?"

Large kitchens (3,000 square feet and up) tend to have space for a certain number of manufacturers. If you don't get a meeting with a co-packer, it could be because they're at capacity in their facility.

2. Number of employees

A typical co-packer is made up of 35 employees. I explain who below, but bring it up as a concern because you may need more than one person to help co-pack for you. In my experience, it's taken a team of 3 people to make 80 gallons of mustard sometimes 4 or 5 if the facility is under a time crunch.

Does the kitchen you're looking at have enough employees?

It's something to consider. Are you going to hop in and help if something goes wrong? I've helped on several productions because it's my company on the line.

We needed products to meet large purchase orders. As a small producer, you hope for enough team members, but sometimes it doesn't happen.

Ask about part time help.

Does the co-packer you're looking at bring in help when they need it or are you responsible for finding extra help? One co-packer I know has an army of part time workers who are called on when she needs help the most.

All of them are great people willing to lend a hand. Truth is, the kitchen manager isn't going to always be the only one handling your product. That means you should meet as many people as possible when you go for a tour.

Now, on to who typically makes up a co-packer's staff:

General Manager

This is the person who runs the show. They were likely instrumental in getting funding to open the facility. They know if you'll fit in the schedule. And they have a general outlook on the industry.

Kitchen Manager

Sometimes the same person as the General Manager. The Kitchen Manager is the one who oversees and participates in all of the productions, 5 days a week. They know how to make every product, how much product they can make in an 8 hour day, and if you'll be able to produce your product on the equipment currently in the kitchen.

FOODTRUCKEMPIRE

It's also likely this person is ServSafe certified (mandatory for third party certified kitchens more on that later in the list).

Food Scientist

These guys are the brains behind the operation. They know everything there is to know about food processing from pH to fill temperature, acidified foods, to scaling recipes. They're knowledge is indispensable. Make sure someone knows something about food science at the co-packing facility.

12 production assistants

Need help weighing out ingredients, filling or labeling product? These people handle all the nitty gritty at the facility even washing the dishes. As mentioned above, there may be more than 2 of these people because they rotate in and out.

Small Business Advisors (optional)

One of the leading shared kitchen & co-packing incubators in Vermont has a small business development liason's office in the building. This is super helpful to producers because now they have business planning and consulting (free, I might add) at their disposal. While this is likely to not be a position in many co-packing facilities, business management cannot be overlooked.

3. Production capability

How many units can the facility pump out in a day? Would they have to produce every day to meet your demand? If they do, it's not a good fit. But, make sure they can produce on a regular schedule. The last you want is to be stuck with no product and purchase orders out your ears with no available kitchen time.

Plus, look at what equipment they have.

Do you need to furnish any special equipment to produce your product? Or, does the kitchen have everything you could ever dream of? Make sure to ask specific questions about equipment. And if they don't have something you need, see if you need to buy it outright or if the facility would be willing to purchase one for you if you sign a year long contract. (More on that in the pricing section later).

Production capacity is important because you may be growing, too. What starts out as 50 cases of product a month may double or triple (like it did for me). That means you need to find a facility that can grow with you not just one for your current needs. Keep that in mind.

4. Distance from your home

Pretty sure you don't want to drive hours to your co-packing space. That would be crazy on so many fronts.

That means, you need to take proximity into account.

Find a kitchen that's close by. Otherwise you'll feel like all you do is drive back and forth wasting both time and money. Two resources that are limited, right?

On a personal note, **we used to drive an hour each way to our first co-packer.**I chose to drop or ship all of my ingredients (to avoid a fee you'll learn more about later). Sometimes, that meant driving back and forth 23 days a week. That ate up a lot of time I could have used to sell more product.

Currently, we're 15 minutes from our co-packer. It's made all the difference. I can coordinate more local deliveries of perishable product, if there's an emergency, it's easier for me to fix it, and well, the most obvious advantage being that my product is closer to me if I need it.

For some of you, you may have to drive long distances. On the plus side, the gas can be written off as a business expense, but don't you want to be able to have time to build your company? Then travel distance should be taken into account when selecting a co-packer.

5. Receiving capability

Your ingredients, labels, and packaging have to make it to the kitchen, right? Figuring out how that happens is important when you're selecting a co-packer. Here's a couple receiving tips/questions to keep in mind:

Is someone always there?

Not only do you frustrate the UPS delivery man when no one is at your co-packer, but it's frustrating for you, too. Make sure you know when and where to have deliveries dropped off. Why so important?

Think about this: if you have a refrigerated or frozen product being delivered, it has to stay at a certain temperature. Your butter or eggs can't be left outside in the summer that would just cost you a ton of money.

Do they have a forklift?

This is going to be kitchen dependent. If the kitchen is less than 3,000 sq ft, it's likely there's no room for a forklift. But, if you're getting a pallet of all purpose flour delivered, you probably don't

want to move it bag by bag. That's why a forklift comes in handy. You can transport product from one end of the kitchen to the other.

Is there a loading dock?

Chances are you're going to have to bring in a lot more raw materials than at your previous kitchen. That makes a loading dock handy. Large semi-trucks can pull up to the receiving area and simply slide a pallet off their truck. Without a loading dock, you have to request a liftgate from the trucking company and there's an extra fee for the liftgate. But, it makes your new co-packer super happy when they don't have to climb onto the truck to disassemble a pallet with over 300 cases of glass jars (Yep I've been there!).

Bottom line: Get a liftgate on the delivery truck or ask if there's a loading dock at your co-packing kitchen.

How do deliveries work?

Many co-packers are logistical nightmares. There's deliveries coming in daily, product being made daily, and employees needed to handle large drop offs. That's why it's smart to learn how deliveries work at the co-packer.

Can they only come on certain days? Are there weight restrictions? And what about deliveries that take up all of your storage space?

It's best to iron out these details before you sign anything. That way you know exactly what you're getting into. For example, at my current co-packer it requires a little more leg work, but I don't pay a premium for it because I'm doing the extra work even with deliveries. It's important though you'll be sending materials to the kitchen all the time. It's best to know how it works.

6. Pricing structure

This is its own section later in the guide, but I'll give you the quick version now. Co-packing pricing can be some of the most confusing pricing you'll ever see. It's not as simple as a $99 one time fee or buy one get one free. It gets much crazier.

How co-packers price their service

There are two main ways co-packers price. The first way is a flat day rate. It could be anywhere from a couple hundred bucks all the way up to $1,000 or more. This is the way I started out at my first co-packer. I paid a day rate. That forced me to crank out as many units as I could on each day. Why? Because the more units I produced, the lower my labor rate was. It's the only cost factor I could leverage.

FOODTRUCKEMPIRE

The other way to charge is a per unit price. This is often figured out after you and your co-packer meet to go over how your product is produced, how many people it takes, is there downtime, do things sit overnight, etc. Based on time involved (including prep), your unit price may fluctuate as I'll discuss later. Per unit pricing is nice because you can predict your unit costs more accurately.

Where many co-packers get you

There are all sorts of fees when you start to work with co-packers. Everything from receiving fees to consulting and storage. Again, these are listed out later in the guide.

Work through your numbers early

Whatever pricing gets handed to you when you engage with a co-packer, make sure you work through the numbers to see if you're still going to make money. You do want to make money, right?

If you're going to be producing a guaranteed amount, you may want to look into contracting so that you get a flat rate throughout the year. It's not only about the price of your product when it leaves the warehouse, but it also means your profit margins throughout the distribution channel.

7. Owner & employee personality

If I had to highlight an item on this list with stars and big giant arrows, it's this one. You have got to get along with your copacker. They're basically married to you. You spend time with them, you have hard conversations, and you are in constant communication. You've got to be nice to them, just like they have to be nice to you or things get rocky.

And, I know sometimes, you won't know someone's true colors until a few months (or maybe years) down the road. It's hard to gauge someone's personality from an hour-long meeting. That's why you should make sure you could work with this person.

Let me tell you a quick story:

My first co-packer started out as a great relationship. She was nice, attentive, and got the job done (albeit at a pricey rate). But, months in, my phone calls weren't being returned, errors were being made in production (costing me more money), and I felt pushed aside for larger contracts they were dealing with.

Lesson learned? Make sure you'd jump in front of a bus for your co-packer. They have your baby, your recipes, in their hands. Make sure it's someone you mesh with, you trust and you can openly communicate with. Funny, sounds a little bit like marriage, doesn't it?

8. Shipping capability

Producing a lot of product means you're moving a lot of product, too. And that means your co-packer has to keep up with what's being shipped where. Some co-packers take care of your finished product leaving the kitchen others don't. Why is this important?

You may need a pallet moved, an online order packed up, or a couple cases shipped off to a regional retailer. Find out if your copacker does this. If they do, it's likely going to cost you either per shipment, case, or unit. The alternative, however, is you picking up all the product and shipping it yourself tons of time so figure out if it's worth it or not for you.

What do I do?

I pick up all of my manufactured product and store it in my basement. I use my co-packer as a pickup location for distributors. I take care of direct orders, online shipments, and events and festivals. Plus, I know how much of each variety I have onhand.

9. Third-party certifications (and health inspections)

The last thing you want to do is produce your product in a kitchen that isn't up to code or worse it's just plain dirty. Check for cleanliness and other health records showing your potential facility has been cleaned. And while you're at it, check for other certifications.

There are tons of health and allergen related permits and certifications. From gluten free to kosher and organic, the list is endless. And you want to find out if your co-packer is certified.

But, be careful. Some facilities may call themselves gluten free and not be certified. That means you can't put gluten free on your label. It has to be from a certified facility. But, more on that later we're getting off topic.

These certifications make it so that many companies are able to lay claim to the many "free statements." But the certifications don't end there.

Your facility also has to abide by state and FDA guidelines. For example, in Vermont, the department of health requires every manufacturer (not just the kitchen) be certified. That means the local health inspector needs to see your production process and make sure the facility is in tiptop shape. And your co-packer is going to have you fit the bill because it's a lot of time and money to get ready for inspections. Time your copacker could be using to make someone else's product.

Another reason you want to check up on third party audits and certifications is it may depend on your company's growth. Whole Foods, one of the major grocery store chains requires your product be produced in a third party certified kitchen. No certification? No Whole Foods.

Make sure the kitchen has proof of certification before you move forward yes, it's that important!

10. Other customer experiences

Let's say you just moved to town and you're looking for the best pizza around. What would you do? Check online? Find Yelp reviews? Or, would you ask your trusting friends and family? The testimonial and experience of others probably heavily influences your decision of where to grab the best pizza ever. Because your friends know the good hangouts and the places to avoid.

The same is true with co-packers. You'll learn a lot about the kitchen from the companies that already produce their products there. But, how do you find out *who* produces there? Just ask.

See if your co-packer will give you contact information to other manufacturers. Ask how long they've been producing there and see if you could get in touch with them. And what should you ask them?

Here are a couple questions to ask:

1. Have you had any challenges with co-packing?

Food producers are honest people. They'll tell you if it's been challenging co-packing. Sure, it may change your opinion or co-packing, but what better way to find out about co-packing than asking people who already do it?

2. What's it like working with the kitchen manager?

Again, honesty here is great, too. Kitchen managers are typically one or the other good or bad. Other producers will let you know which one their manager is. And hopefully it's good. Keep in mind, the kitchen manager may only give you success stories not other producers who may give you the honest truth. Get to know them through other people and then make your own decision.

3. Would you change anything about the facility?

No co-packer is perfect there's flaws in every facility. Talk to other producers to find out what your potential copacker's weaknesses are. Maybe it's hard to make deliveries or schedule a production. Producers will tell you what's wrong the facility (and what they'll do the

4. Are you able to produce to demand?

You want to know if there are any production bottlenecks, right? And what about producing to meet a spike in sales? What if you have a huge press hit and product is flying out the door? You

 FOODTRUCKEMPIRE

want to know if your co-packer will be able to meet the demand. Other customers will have a good gauge for this based on their own experiences.

11. Equipment needs

You can expect the majority of co-packers to have the same standard equipment. From a six burner stove to a kettle, kitchen wares to a three bay sink, there are certain pieces of equipment a commercial kitchen needs. But, let's explore the equipment that would make your co-packing experience easier (and cheaper).

Here's a list of the "nice to haves" in a co-packing kitchen:

Large kettles

You're not going to be able to produce the product you need with a stock pot or even a 5 gallon tabletop kettle. Co-packers should have at least one 40gallon kettle (or two 20 gallon kettles like my current co-packer). This allows you to make enough product and justify the additional cost of co-packing. After all, you should be moving some serious product if you're considering co-packing.

Commercial Immersion Blender

Definitely kettle's best friend right here. Stop mixing ingredients with a paddle (those are necessary, too) and pick up a commercial immersion blender. But, be careful, this thing blends like no other.

Oh, and if you don't want everything coming together (meaning, you still need chunks of something like tomatoes), stick with the good old fashioned paddle. Sidenote: another added benefit of commercial blenders? Awesome biceps. It's pretty heavy so you might want to hit the gym for some arm curls. Ok, I kid, I kid.

Automatic (or pedal powered) filler for dry and wet

I think filling machines are cooler than any home kitchen appliance. They save an incredible amount of time and keep your product's net fill weight as close to what's on the label as possible. Gone are the days of hand filling your product.

If co-packers don't have an automatic filler, check for a pedal powered one. All that means is the filler is activated by stepping on a pedal with your foot to fill each jar. This is more likely at smaller co-packers.

Labeling machine (there are tons out there)

I have a confession to make: Our products are still hand labeled. Yes, my co-packer is tiny and they haven't invested in a labeling machine.

And yes, that means your co-packer should have one. Hand labeling takes forever and sometimes the labels don't go on straight. While labeling machines aren't perfect either, they certainly help to speed things up. And when you're producing over 1,000 units a day, believe me, you want as much automation as possible. Viva la labeler!

Horizontal and/or Vertical Band Sealer

It was like Christmas when this arrived at my house a few years ago. We purchased a horizontal band sealer off eBay for my energy bar company. It helped us package 500 bars a day from our home kitchen. Sure, it broke a few times and required some black electrical tape, but the seal was great, the small conveyor belt sped things up, and we were cranking. Make sure your co-packer has one of these if you're manufacturing any bagged items that need to be sealed like nuts, granola, cereals, or dry mixes. It will save your life. Guaranteed.

There's tons more equipment that should make it onto the "nice-to-haves" list, but we've got to move on to answering another question:

What if your co-packer doesn't have the equipment you need?

While I hope this doesn't happen to you, you may find co-packers in your area don't have the equipment you need. Don't panic. It happens all the time. They simply haven't produced a product like yours. Here are three options to remedy the situation:

1. Have the co-packer purchase the equipment

While unlikely, you might be able to get your co-packer to purchase the equipment for you. Why? Because it likely benefits them. They're able to bring in more producers because they have the equipment. Plus, it'll help get your product produced faster. Keep in mind the co-packer will likely want to have you sign a year-long contract before they purchase equipment for you. That way, they know they'll have a consistent revenue stream from you and be able to justify the added expense.

2. Split the cost with your co-packer

I've done this one and it's worked out great. When we switched co-packers, the new place didn't have a commercial immersion blender (see above about why it's so awesome). I explained the benefits to the kitchen manager and we agreed to split it. Now, it's used by almost every

producer and is a great addition to the kitchen's equipment line up. This is the best way to go if you don't have the funds to buy the equipment outright.

3. Finance the equipment yourself

And probably the most popular way to get new equipment in the door, financing equipment yourself is likely to happen at some point. Co-packers don't want to take the risk on you, they might not have the room, and just like you, they may not have the cash flow to split the purchase. Here are a couple tips if you're looking to finance equipment yourself:

- Shop around look for used equipment at auctions or restaurant equipment stores.
- Test the equipment especially used. You want to know it works before you bring it in.
- Loan options from crowdfunding to bank loans, and credit cards, explore your options.

I'm not a banker, but if you can finance a piece of equipment to make your life easier (for you and your co-packer), I'd do it. Worst case scenario is you re-sell the equipment if it isn't right for you.

Remember, you don't have to cut ties with your co-packer if they don't have the equipment you need. Make it work by using some of the strategies above. On to the final point.

12. Scheduling production

Wouldn't it be horrible if you had outstanding purchase orders you couldn't fill? It'd be even worse if you couldn't get kitchen time to meet demand, wouldn't it? Obviously, you can't plan for every spike in demand, but it's something to consider when selecting your co-packer. Here are a few questions to ask when you meet with your co-packer:

- How many units of my product can you produce in a day?
- How many days in advance should I schedule my productions?
- What happens if I need to change or cancel a production?
- Is there a community calendar to see when there is kitchen time available?

Again, while it's not an exhaustive list, it's important to know how co-packers run their kitchens. The last thing you want to have happen is have no kitchen time in the middle of your busy season. That means plan ahead.

Tip: Look at your previous year's sales. Forecast an increase and schedule more productions when you're at your peak.

Just like buying a house, the requirements list to select a co-packer is daunting (and to think this isn't an end all be all list).

 FOODTRUCKEMPIRE

Also, don't pick the first co-packing kitchen you tour. There could be better kitchens that suit your company's needs. For example, I should have looked further before choosing my first co-packer. She ended up far too large for us. That mistake cost us several thousand dollars.

Don't make the same mistake I did.

I've seen many food businesses crash and burn because of strained co-packer relationships. Their product isn't the same, quality drops, and you not only have an upset producer, you have a frustrated co-packer. Not a good mix, my friend, not a good mix.

Credibility of your co-packer is more important than price.

You're *marrying* your co-packer. The only difference? There's no ring. But there's months of planning, people to talk to, and of course you want the event to go off without a hitch.

How do I know my co-packer is credible?

Credibility is something you want in your bank, your contractor, your life insurance provider, and your accountant. But, you also want your co-packer to be credible. It's not just a one off relationship. You are likely going to be talking to your co-packer several times a week making sure everything is ontrack.

The last thing you want is for something to go wrong.

For example, your recipes get leaked, too much of an ingredient goes in the kettle, or you're overcharged on your last invoice.

5 Ways to know your co-packer is the real deal

1. They ask for your scheduled process documents

Your scheduled process documents are like a certificate of occupancy for your home. It lets you live there (or gives you access to the co-packer's kitchen). Without them, the co-packer won't know *how* to produce your product. Sure, you have a recipe, but what about the process? Good co-packers make sure you have a scheduled process. That way your product comes out the same way every time.

2. They sign a non-disclosure agreement

Button up your legal documents before you agree to any co-packing. And one of the most important is a NDA or a nondisclosure agreement. What this does is protects you and your co-packer from leaking or sharing your recipe. Because we all know if Grandma's blueberry jam

recipe gets out, it's all over. Protect yourself. And the true sign of a great co-packer is someone who covers the legal bases first before you step foot in the door.

3. They produce for large companies and brands

It's like social proof for the food industry. Large brands produce with reputable companies. For example, my first co-packer packed for King Arthur Flour and Purely Elizabeth: both companies I'd heard of. My second co-packer produced for much smaller brands, but I found this led to more credibility because she was a small producer herself. But, be warned: large companies may sound cool, but the kitchen might not be the best fit for your company.

4. They are upfront about costs and additional fees

All I can think of is a used car salesman who sells you the car for a flat fee and then tacks on hidden fees and charges. You don't want to buy a car from him! And you definitely do not want to work with a co-packer who willy nilly throws line items on your invoice. You need to know the costs upfront and if there are any other potential fees you *could* incur while producing at the kitchen.

5. They view you as a partner, not just a blank check

Co-packers need to make money. But, they should be your friend, too. A lot of people are in business for the money (which ironically may never come in the copious amounts they hope it does). But, genuine, credible co-packers are there to help you through the tough times, solve your food production problems, and be your business partner. Sure, it helps that you pay on time, but keep this in mind as you search for a co-packer. You want a partner.

With credibility in check, it's time to find out what these co-packing facilities are all about. You can find information on their websites and by touring the facility. Let's explore how to get in touch with your potential co-packers and learn more about them.

Narrow your list down to 1 - 3 possible copackers.

If you're lucky, you've got a variety of co-packers to choose from. If you do, narrow them down to 13 and go through this co-packer evaluation process below. You won't be wasting your time and you'll ask all the right questions:

1. Do a phone interview first

Don't get in your car, drive an hour, and meet with your chosen co-packers quite yet. They could be the wrong fit. You wouldn't want to waste all that money and time would you? That's why I recommend starting with a phone interview. That way, you're comfortable, at your desk, and have your list of questions in front of you. Oh, and speaking of questions...

2. Ask the hard questions

This is your food product we're talking about. You don't want to have any surprises when it comes to figuring out who to choose to produce it. That would be a lot of regret, wouldn't it. You want to make sure you make the right selection. Ask the tough questions:

How do you process a product recall?

You don't want any joking around or laziness when it comes to product recalls. Make sure they have a process in place that they follow and product can be recalled within an hour. Many kitchens with third party certifications are usually quick because they have systems (and software) in place to help you with a recall. It's likely it won't happen, but you want to be sure there's a process in place if it does.

Have you had any production errors occur and what did you do to correct them?

This is a big one for me because of personal experiences, but it could happen to you too. Ask them if they've screwed up. This tells you if they're honest and handle situations well while under pressure. It's fine if they're able to refocus from the error, but did they communicate with the client when it happened or did they wait until production was completed?

Will I be notified of price increases before being invoiced?

It all comes down to money. Before you're blindsided by price increases or mysterious line items on your invoice, ask to be notified about price increases as soon as possible. That way, if you need to look for a new co-packer you can. Know what you're being charged for and find out if your co-packer is upfront about it.

Who pays for the third-party inspections?

Remember all of those inspections I talked about earlier? Well, they're expensive. And it's important to outline who pays for the inspection. Is it the co-packer? The producer? Or can it be multiple producers? Find this out earlier rather than later as it may be a determining factor in your selection. Unplanned inspections are costly to small food companies.

Is there a contract I need to sign?

To get started with many co-packers, you'll need to sign a contract. Make sure the contract contains a nondisclosure agreement (NDA) which protects your co-packer from stealing your secret recipes. The contract may only be put in the table if you're looking for better rates and agree to produce a certain amount.

That means, if you agree to produce 100 days of the year, your co-packer will likely give you a price break because their facility is guaranteed to be full because of you. As always, read the

contract over a few times to make sure you're not being taken advantage of. Be cautious of upfront fees, additional charges, and what happens with breach of contract.

What other fees are associated with making my product?

Speaking of different fees, there are several and they're all discussed at length later in the book. Make sure all of these fees are outlined for you before you sign your contract. Often these fees come as a surprise to many manufacturers and it hurts their profit margins. Even if you don't expect to pay them when you start, expect to pay them within your first year of co-packing.

3. Go for a visit and bring a foodie friend.

Just like searching for a college, you toured campus, spoke with representatives, and asked questions about campus life. Touring a co-packing facility is the same experience. Except, this time, you don't want to bring your parents along. Instead, bring another food producer or someone who knows the ins and outs of the industry.

Why would you bring along someone?

Generally, food entrepreneurs have this sense about each other. They know who to trust and who not to trust.

If you know a food entrepreneur, ask them to come with you. They'll be honest with you and the co-packer. If you won't ask the hard questions, they will. Here's what to look for when you visit your shortlist of co-packers.

What to look for when you visit:

1. Everything on pallets

Things strewn all over the floor are not up to code. All ingredients and other materials need to be kept off the floor. The easiest way for co-packers to do this is use a combination of pallets and metal shelves. Kind of like Costco or BJ's.

2. Lot tracking documents

Ask to see that your co-packer uses a lot tracking system. Whether it's pen and paper or a large enterprise piece of software, see that lot tracking is being completed. While your co-packer doesn't have to show you another manufacturer's documents, just have them show you the printouts they use. If they don't participate in lottracking, you're going to have a tough time recalling product, should that happen.

3. HACCP Plans and Good Manufacturing Practices (GMP's)

I know, this is the boring stuff (well, exciting to some). Make sure your co-packer is HACCP certified (this includes everything from receiving ingredients to shipping finished product out of the facility) and practices good manufacturing practices.

They likely do if they maintain any third party certifications. Ask to see documentation if you don't see clipboards around the kitchen document processes and critical control points.

4. Hairnets/hats and gloves

It sounds so basic. Wouldn't all food processing facilities use hairnets and gloves? You'd think so, but some skip over the easy things that keep your food product safe. I've been in facilities that don't use hairnets and gloves and I've also been in facilities that have all guests wear chef's jackets, hair nets, and gloves.

Plus, they have you sanitize your shoes in a footbath as you enter the kitchen (this was a large commercial facility). Keep in mind, all facilities are different and have to abide by different regulations based on the certifications and inspections they have. A head covering and gloves are requirements and this may be included in the GMP's from above.

5. General cleanliness

Again, obvious. But, a clean kitchen means you're witnessing a well oiled machine. The floors should be clean of debris, the sinks shiny, and the shelves organized. Ask if the kitchen is cleaned and washed down after every production. The last thing you want is remnants from another product in your product, just to push units out the door.

6. Updated equipment

Old stuff breaks. New stuff (hopefully) doesn't. Try to find out when the equipment at your prospective co-packer was brought in and when it may be replaced. Old equipment may break more easily than new equipment. And for that reason, you want updated equipment. Remember you get what you pay for, too.

7. Proper storage

If there's anything I've learned, it's that co-packers never seem to have enough storage. And they charge for it if they're tight on space (see the part about hidden expenses later in the guide).

Storage is important because you want to know the co-packer can handle your growth. When you order a couple hundred cases of glass, it needs a place to go. The same for all of your ingredients. Make sure your co-packer has some room to spare (even if you have to pay for it).

8. Good rapport between the kitchen manager and employees

How do employees interact with each other? How do they interact with their manager? The relationship between employee and manager is crucial because you don't want an employee sabotaging your production just because they aren't happy with their boss. Look for open body language, laughing/joking, and employees who respect their manager.

While there's a lot more to look for, these 7 things are the most important. They make a huge difference between which co-packers move to the top of the list and which fall to the bottom.

Now that you've visited a couple co-packers and seen their kitchens, it's time to evaluate the best co-packer for the job. And it goes far beyond what you like and don't like. Here's a couple things to think about.

Questions to ask yourself after you visit all of your co-packers:

1. Did I get along with the co-packer?

As I've stated earlier, your co-packer is like your significant other. You deal with them almost every day, know their quirks, and their faults. Your co-packer should be just like your best friend. Were they approachable? Did they ask questions about you? Did they introduce you to their employees?

I bet you enjoy working with nice people. People with integrity. Evaluate how you felt talking to the kitchen manager. If they weren't the right fit, that's your first red flag move on.

2. Were there any warning signs?

What didn't you like about the kitchen? Were there things the kitchen needed to work on? If there were any warning signs, are they able to be worked through with you or the co-packer? You have to be able to start off on the right foot. Otherwise, it won't be a great relationship.

3. Can I grow with this company?

As noted by the need for lots of storage, the co-packers needs to have the ability to grow with you. Otherwise, you'll be looking for a new co-packer in a short period of time. That's something we'll talk about later, too. With any company that gets started, you expect to grow. Find a co-packer who is willing to grow with you.

4. Are they able to produce anything else besides my type of product?

This is thinking ahead a little bit, but does the co-packer have the ability to produce anything else? Just because you make spaghetti sauce, doesn't mean you won't start making seasoning mixes, garlic bread, and pizza sauce. Having a co-packer with a diverse product mix means it's easier for you to expand your product line.

5. Are the costs associated reasonable to produce my product?

When you tour a co-packing facility, you'll likely go over all of the costs associated with co-packing (and there are a lot). What it comes to is can you afford it? You may have stumbled on the best facility in a 200mile radius, but do you have enough cash in the bank to do a run? As you'll learn later, when I started out, I almost ran my bank account to $0 and it was frightening.

Now that we're on the topic money, it's time to get down to numbers. The costs of co-packing can either be straight forward or complex. I've dealt with both. And the hard part is every co-packer is different.

Let's explore the finances of co-packing below.

How much does it cost to work with a co-packer?

After visiting and talking with several co-packers, it's time to take a hard look at the numbers. You need to know if you're going to make money. After all, why would you co-pack if you're going to lose money, right?

There are three ways co-packers charge. All of them have their pros and cons. While you may be able to work out a deal with your co-packer, generally fees are fees unless you sign an annual or multi-year contract.

While this section is quite numbers heavy with several examples, I'll try my best to make it simple for you. I'm not a big fan of numbers either.

Take a deep breath and dive in!

Three ways co-packers Charge:

The three ways co-packers charge are meant to meet the needs of every manufacturer. Sometimes the rates are determined on a case-by-case basis, but many co-packers keep their fees the same just to maintain their own sanity.

1. Flat Day Rate

This is simple. One flat fee for the entire day. For example, each day you produce costs you $500. This means you need to produce as many units as possible in that 8hour day to reduce your per unit labor cost.

2. Per Unit Rate

Also simple. You pay per unit produced. Usually this is somewhere between $0.25 - $0.50. Anything higher, and you likely won't make any money.

3. Per Hour Rate

If your production only takes a half day or you need extra help, you may get offered an hourly rate. Rates of $25 - $80/hour are typically depending on the equipment you use.

The most common fees are flat day rate and per unit. It's rare to see a per hour rate unless you're just doing prep for production and there isn't a whole lot of finished goods.

Something to note here:

You could also lock in a contracted rate. If you're new and can't guarantee demand (like many small food producers), you'll likely be stuck with a day rate that won't go any lower.

Co-packers do that because they're unsure of your likelihood to stick around. Most food companies are gone within a few years. However, if you're a large company with consistent production runs, you're more likely to get a contract with lower rates.

While we're on the subject of contracts and lower rates....

Let's talk about the fees you probably didn't come across when talking with co-packers. Just like the house analogy from earlier, if you're buying a house that seems too good to be true, it probably is. There could be hidden damage which would cost you thousands of dollars.

Same with co-packers.

A day rate is just one part of the fees you incur. As co-packers become more in demand, they're looking for every possible way to make money. After all, they don't seem to be in short supply of possible food manufacturers, do they?

Below, you'll find a short list of fees that you could rack up while working with a co-packer. It's important to keep these in mind when you're selecting someone to work with. Often, these costs aren't associated with manufacturing though. But, your net profit margin takes a hit when you add in the unexpected operating costs.

 FOODTRUCKEMPIRE

188

Here we go....

The hidden fees most co-packers won't tell you about

1. Receiving fees

Even if you source and ship your ingredients to the co-packer, they may still charge you to receive your product. For example, when I would ship glass jars to my first co-packer, they would charge me $20 to receive it. Turns out, I was charged that amount for anything received by them. From that point on (with the exception of glass), I hand delivered everything. Look for receiving fees to be around $25 for each delivery.

2. Ingredient prep fees

This one makes sense (to me), but make sure you incorporate it. Ingredient prep is typically charged by the hour. Let's say you use fresh peppers. Well, your copacker isn't going to give you time for free to prep them, are they? This either leads you to use ingredients that require less prep (or not prep at all) or consider raising your prices to incorporate this added cost. Prep fees typically run $25 - $50/hour because the facility not only has to cover labor cost, but they have to make some money, too.

3. Pallet storage fees

Space is a hot commodity in co-packing. And co-packers charge for it, too. Mainly because many food entrepreneurs (probably yourself included) don't have the room to store 50# bags of sugar, a pallet of glass, and thousands of units of finished product. What's it typically cost? Be prepared to pay between $25 and $100/month per pallet. The rate goes up when you're looking for refrigerated or frozen storage.

4. Consulting time

Unfortunately, you can't pick your co-packer's brain forever (I know, wouldn't that be great?) That means your next invoice might have a line item for consulting on it. Whether you talked about pH, HACCP, or distribution strategy, consulting is a good chunk of change. Fees range from $50 - $250/hour for food consultants.

5. Third Party Fees

Third party audits, required for shelf space at many major grocery chains, cost a ton of money upwards of $2,000. If you're the only producer looking for the certification, you're likely to be footing the bill. You're lucky if 2 or 3 manufacturers need the certification because you can split it. And the other certifications like gluten free, nongmo, and kosher, all cost money, too. Not only is this a cost you should plan for, but watch for it on invoices from your co-packer as well.

 **FOODTRUCK**EMPIRE

6. Order Fulfillment Fees

Shooting over an email with a purchase order is easy just hit send. But, for your co-packer it takes time to process your order, get it packed up, and put on the truck. Plus, it takes them away from other activities (like making more product). If your co-packer offers order fulfilment, be prepared to pay a flat rate plus a per case rate of $0.25- $0.50.

7. Ingredient Sourcing Fees

There are co-packers out there who will help you through the entire production process, including ordering all of your ingredients. Yes, they do exist. Ordering all of your ingredients is tedious and can take hours if you have a lot of products. Outsourcing this to your co-packer is an option. There's likely going to be a delivery rate (see above) and a percent markup 1020%. The big question is, are you willing to have 1020% increase in your raw materials cost for someone else to pick up the phone or order online? It's a fee I personally opted out of, but other companies are willing to pony up the big bucks.

8. Cleanup Fees

Does your product make the kitchen look like a disaster zone? Then you might need to pay cleanup fees to get the kitchen back to normal before the next production. I haven't seen it happen with copackers too much, but this happens a lot with shared commercial kitchens.

9. Casing Your Product

For many food companies who order bottles and jars (many of you) to package their product, it's often the case where a case box doesn't come with the glass. That means every 12 or every 6 units needs to go in it's own box, labeled, and taped up. That'll cost you, too. $0.50/case usually.
While many of these (with the exception of ingredient prep and ordering fees) are operational costs and not directly related to the manufacturing of your product, they should be taken into consideration.

If you're charged for all of these "hidden" fees, you're likely looking at an additional $300 - $500/month in expenses. If you're growing, it's an investment. But, if you're just starting out, look at ways to cut costs and avoid paying these fees.

Now, let's look at some examples:

Here's the background: You make jelly and need to find a co-packer to produce 1,000 units. Let's look at each scenario above, with a mix of fees thrown in.

 FOODTRUCKEMPIRE

Flat Day Rate:

- Day rate: $750 for an 8 hour day
- Units produced: 1,000
- Cost per unit: $0.75

That's pretty high for production. But, let's make it a bit more complicated. Let's say you had three shipments received for that production and you had a couple of prep hours the night before:

- Day rate: $750 for an 8 hour day
- Receiving fees: $60
- Ingredient prep: $100
- Units produced: 1,000
- Cost per unit: $0.91

Your labor cost per unit just increased 21.3%

And that's just your labor cost. Nevermind your ingredients, packaging, transportation costs, and other fees. The increase needs to be passed all the down your distribution channel, up to your customer or you'll be making less money.

What are the downsides to paying a flat day rate?

1. Fluctuating per unit rate

Every time you produce, you have no idea how much your labor is going to influence your product cost. One week, your product is cheap to produce. The next? Something goes wrong and your cost spikes. It's tough to control.

2. Pressure to produce as much as you can

When I was just starting out, I was paying a flat day rate. That meant I needed to produce close to 1,000 units just to break even. And I didn't have the demand to meet the supply. When I produced less, my costs went up. It's just part of the numbers game.

3. Tight cash flow

When you pay several hundred dollars a day for use of a co-packing facility and you're doing it weekly, it adds up. Then you've got jars, caps, ingredients, transportation, and time. That's a lot

of money. Some production runs have cost me upwards of $2,500. And that was just to get off the ground.

Per unit pricing

This is the pricing model my co-packer currently uses. It allows for greater flexibility, based on demand of your product. That means you can make 10 cases of one product and 5 of another. Let's look into it further.

Per unit price is typically $0.30$0.80/unit depending on your process.

If you have a lot of manual labor attached to your products (like preparing fresh produce, hand filling, hand labeling, etc) your per unit rate will be higher.

Let's look at an example:

- Units produced: 1,000
- Cost per unit: $0.30
- Prep of ingredients: 2 hours at $30/hour = $60
- Total labor cost: $0.36/unit or $360

See how your labor rate, even with added prep is almost half the cost of a day rate? Now, assuming your ingredients aren't too expensive, you've got an opportunity to make money here. This means you can go to retailers and distributors and be confident about your pricing structure.

Now, this is not to say that flat day rate doesn't work. It does. It works for larger companies who are able to produce in volume. If you're just getting started, try to find a co-packer who will produce your product using per unit pricing.

What are the downsides to per unit pricing?

May require production minimums

Your copacker isn't going to make a case of your product. They're going to require a minimum production yield. Why? Because they need to have a certain volume in the kettle so that it functions properly. For example, a 20gallon kettle requires at least 3 gallons of ingredients to properly heat and produce product.

Preptime may be an added expense

You can assume that per unit pricing is a baseline cost of doing business. Then, there's likely to be prep time and other fees like I described above. Yes, this increases your per unit price, but it's likely to still be less than flat day rate.

Per hour rate

While rare, it's also possible that co-packers charge a per hour rate. This is good for companies with fast productions and little cash.

If a shared kitchen is producing your product for you or helping you during production an hourly rate is likely applied.

Let's look at an example:

- Units produced: 1,000
- Workers used: 2
- Hourly charge: $25/hour
- Hours: 5
- Total labor cost: $0.25/unit or $250

Now, there's one big distinction here: You're in the kitchen, too. Let's add your labor into the mix so that you have 3 people producing product at $25/hour. (If you value your time at more money, you can increase the number).

- Units produced: 1,000
- Workers used: 3 (including yourself)
- Hourly charge: $25/hour
- Hours: 5
- Total labor cost: $0.375/unit or $375

Just by adding yourself into the labor mix (because you would have to pay a third person if you weren't there), you increased your labor cost by $0.12/unit.

And another question you're probably asking....

Why are you hiring people for $25/hour? The people helping you work for the facility. They know how to use the equipment. They know how to abide by HACCP guidelines. They're worth it! Your actual charge may be less in some scenarios.

That's the quick summary of co-packing costs. With cost under your belt, it's time to make a selection. You've talked to many co-packers on the phone. You've toured their facility and nailed down all costs associated.

Don't just pick one.

This is a strategic decision for your company just as much as it's a financial one. Take time to sit down and think about which facility you're going to select and why. It's truly a make or break moment.

Once you've made your decision, there's lots to do. Let's take a look at what's needed to get the ball rolling with your co-packer.

Selecting a co-packer

Woohoo! You did it. You've made it through the lengthy research process, asked the tough questions, and found a co-packer to work with.

Now, it's time to get ready for day one of production. But before then, there's a couple things you have to cross off your todo list first.

How to make sure you have your bases covered:

1. Notify them of your intent to have product co-packed (call them)

Your co-packer probably won't follow up with you, so give them a call. Let them know you've selected them to co-pack your products. Ask them about next steps and get your paperwork in as soon as possible.

2. Get a nondisclosure agreement signed immediately

Speaking of paperwork, one of the first things you should do is get both parties (your company and the co-packer) to sign an NDA. Sign it before you talk about the process or send your recipes over. The last thing you want is stolen recipes!

3. Make sure you have your suppliers lined up

Moving to a co-packer likely means buying ingredients and supplies in bulk rather than just running to the grocery store. Spend time identifying suppliers who sell your products and cost everything out. Sometimes (believe it or not), ingredients are still going to be less expensive from the grocery store than in bulk. I'm told it's a supply and demand issue. (It's why we still buy vinegar from Costco and get weird looks!)

4. Pad your bank account for unforeseen circumstances

When you start a food business you're often told to see how much money you need and double it. The same is true when moving to a co-packer. You never know what could go wrong or if you need extra money for increased production. Make sure there's a couple extra thousand dollars just in case something happens and you didn't plan on it.

With your co-packer lined up, legal out of the way, suppliers located, and money in the bank, you're ready to enter the fun filled world of co-packing. Don't worry, I'll walk you through step-by-step and give you solutions to problems you might run into.

Starting to work with your co-packer

It's kind of like the first day of school. You need to have all of your paperwork in order, dressed in the right clothes, and make new friends. And not to mention those lists you get of the stuff your kid needs. If you think of your kid as your company and the list preparar as your co-packer, here's the list of things you need.

What your co-packers needs from you:

1. Scheduled process (optional for some, but recommended for all)

If you make an acidified food (like mustard, jam, pickles, salad dressing), you need a scheduled process. A scheduled process is a document that states your production methods are sound. It also states critical control points, like pH and fill temperature. Scheduled processes can be completed at several college campuses across the US like Cornell, University of Maine, and NC State.

Scheduled processes are needed by your co-packer so they know how to produce your product. Plus, they're going to want to know any "production secrets" you may have like prep of fresh produce, order of operations, etc.

2. Certificate of Insurance

From day one, you should have $1 million in product liability insurance and $2 million in general aggregate. This products you, your products, and your company from a lawsuit (which hopefully

 FOODTRUCKEMPIRE

never happens). You may also have to name your co-packing facility as additionally insured. This is sometimes included in your annual premium. If not, it's $25- $50 per additionally insured party. This protects your co-packer from liability of your products.

3. Your production dates

How often are you going to need space? How much product will you be producing? Should you schedule these dates ahead of time? Communicate all of this to your co-packer because you need to get penciled (err...penned) into their calendar. The last thing you want is to not be able to meet demand because you can't get on your copacker's schedule! That would be killer.

I like to forecast demand (or at least try) 6 months out and schedule productions accordingly. To give you an example of how crazy I am, I have production scheduled for the entire year of 2014 3 months ahead of time. It's better to have more production dates than you need and cancel them than not enough.

4. Information about incoming shipments

I like to provide my kitchen manager with a heads up when big shipments are coming in like hundreds of pounds of mustard powder or pallets of glass. I ask her when a good delivery time would be and order accordingly. This not only helps her to anticipate when large deliveries will be happening, but it's respectful and puts me on good terms.

5. Honest and Open Communication

While this isn't a tangible item, it's incredibly important. Why? Because you could forget to tell your co-packer about a process change or be upset with something and hold a grudge neither are good. I tell my co-packer pretty much everything if it relates to our working relationship. She helps me solve problems and I help her solve problems. The relationship was built on honest and open communication and it should always stay that way.
With all of your paperwork in, you're ready to get your first production run at your new facility under your belt. But, don't just let it happen. Be proactive and show up at your production. See how everything works and where there could be improvements.

Before you walk in that door, here are a couple things to think about before, during, and after you fire up the kettle.

How to make your first co-packing experience a success

Note: You may be using your first production to test and scale up your recipe. This is a critical step if you don't have scaled recipes. From weighing out your ingredients to making sure your spice blends are right when you increase production, **do not skip this step.** Sure, it might cost you money, but it's better to screw up a 5 gallon batch of product than 200, right? Glad we agree there.

FOODTRUCKEMPIRE

Produce what you need:
Similar to above, produce what you need, even if this means an increased per unit cost. Producing excess product puts you in a bind because then you have to sell that product. And if you don't have retailers, distributors, or customers lined up to take the product off your hands, it'll sit there and go past code. Produce to demand. If you need to increase by 1020%, that would be fine, too. That way, you have a little extra in case you get a spike in demand.

Stay calm and collected:
Your first production can quickly put you in a state of frantic hair pulling. Take a deep breath. Your co-packers have years of experience under their belts. You're in good hands. Of course, that doesn't mean problems aren't going to happen.

On my first production day, I brought in the wrong salt (yeah....). I panicked because I needed a significant amount. Luckily salt is cheap and my co-packer has extra on hand. Learn from me. Everything will be ok. You'll get help and figure it out.

Don't critique:

Your co-packer is going to do things differently simply by the nature of who they are and the equipment they're using. Let them work through your recipe.

What you do on your stovetop at home is going to be significantly different to how you make your product in bulk. And you never know, your recipe may end up better in the end because of it. Several of my mustards have better consistency and texture after being made in bulk. All thanks to ideas my kitchen manager had. Watch and learn. Don't critique until you're finished.

Debrief at the end:

When you've cleaned the kitchen up, talk with your production manager and kitchen manager to review what went right and wrong. Bring up the success of the days and areas you think need to be improved either on your end or the co-packers end.

This opens the door with honest communication. While some of it may be tough love, when you drive home you'll be glad you got everything you wanted off your chest.

Your first production is likely to be smaller. This is the time you should work the kinks out. Get ingredients down, production process down, and picking up of finished goods sorted out.

But keep going to your first few productions. Yes, I realize you are paying a co-packer to make your product, so you shouldn't have to be there. But, this is the quality of your product we're talking about. Hear me out:

Here's why you need to go to your co-packing facility for your first three production runs:

Oversee the transition from kitchen to co-packing

If you have several product lines, chances are everything won't be made on the first day. When you're producing a product that's new to the co-packer, it's important to be there if something goes wrong. I've sent several new recipes to my co-packer, scaled up and ready to go, only to find out they were production nightmares. Be there.

Make sure your kitchen manager is producing your product correctly

Wouldn't it be a bummer if you showed up and your product wasn't what you expected it to be? It's happened to me twice. And I'm going to tell you both stories.

Story #1

I wanted to make small jars of mustard. I ordered 4 oz jars that would fit a little bit less mustard in them, so our net wt was actually around 3 oz. My labels said net wt. 3 oz. My jars were filled to 3 oz. And it left a huge gap between the product and the cap. Not only did it create an inefficiency in our process, but I wasn't told about the problem until I came to pick up the product.

What should have been done? I should have received a phone call from my co-packer explaining the problem. The jars could have been filled to the top and labels reprinted. Instead, I awkwardly sold what looked like empty jars of mustard.

Story #2

Oh, our horseradish mustard. It was the best seller (up until we started selling Maple Wholegrain). And then it all changed. I went down to pick up the finished product.

I was met with this "We accidentally double the horseradish, but we think it tastes better anyway." Ok. Panic set in. My costs just increased on the product about 10%.

Plus, this was the way I had to make it moving forward. But, I didn't know about the problem until I had 100 cases of it in the back of my SUV. While it ended up being a good problem to have (people liked the mustard with more horseradish), it still was cause for concern about what else could happen.

What should have been done? Better communication. The recipe should have been scrapped and started over with product made to our specifications. Instead, my co-packer ran with it.

While I certainly hope everything goes smoothly with your co-packing experience, know that it might not. Know that you may have to make decisions on the fly, sprint to the grocery store to remedy the situation, and then go back to complete production.

It's happened to every co-packing food producer I've talked to nothing goes smoothly when you're just starting out. Once you've completed your first couple of runs, everything should be falling into place (unless you have problems like I did!).

This means you get more time to focus on sales, instead of spending time slaving over a hot oven. But, it's important to keep lines of communication open with your co-packer.

As you build trust, credibility, and a better working relationship, your copacker starts to become a lot more than a producer of your product. Let's explore this idea further.

How to establish a better relationship with your co-packer

Co-packers are married to your product. They make it for you. They heat up the kettle, preheat the oven, and package it. And some of them even do all of the ordering of your ingredients. **That's an incredible amount of control for your company.** Putting that much trust into a team can be a frightening experience. And a relationship you don't want to jeopardize.

That's why I wanted to share some tips to make sure you keep your copacker happy:

1. Refer new business

I know you've got at least one goal for your company. I bet it's making money. Am I right? Probably. And the same goes with your co-packer. They're a business, too. So, whenever you're at a farmer's market or chatting up a demo guy at your neighborhood grocery store, keep your co-packer in mind. They'll love you when you refer business their way. Plus, you may even get a discount out of it. Ka-ching!

2. Stay organized

We've all got a million things going on with our food businesses – ordering ingredients, production, shipping online orders, filling purchase orders, trying to land distributors. It's a lot. And you've got to stay organized with everything – especially your copacker. Make sure you communicate when everything will arrive, the amount you'd like to produce, and other important details. That way there's no surprises on production day.

3. Produce with them

I make sure to hop in on a production at least every quarter. I do this to make sure things are going smoothly and product is being manufactured to my standards. You might catch things you don't want to see, but at least you'll be able to nip them in the bud for the next production.

4. Let them about upcoming products

I always give my co-packer advance notice about what we're planning to do next. She typically has a few ideas and gets excited when we launch a new product. For example, when we introduced a holiday mustard in the winter of 2013, I sent over a recipe, but we talked about how the process could be improved. She executed the different process and we ended up with a much better product (and nothing stuck in the filler!).

5. Think about how to make their life easier.

Can you let them know when deliveries are coming? Can you do some of the prep work yourself to save money and prep hours? When you realize all your co-packer does for you, you'll want to return the favor. Be accommodating, send them a holiday card, or make your process easier? They'll appreciate it!

Why work on your relationship?

Aren't co-packers just supposed to make your product? Yes, that's their main priority, however, you want to be on their good side. As Rocky DeCarlo from Rocky's Hot Saucesays:

"Pay the co-packer 50% up front with your order and pay the balance when the product is finished or you pick up your product. Don't be late paying them. Everybody [in any business] likes to get paid ASAP especially when they are laying out there cash for your product. That also gives you some leverage when you need a favor, quick delivery, partial run etc. Nobody likes being a bank for someone else."

You're a food entrepreneur. They're a co-packer. You help each other be successful. Tread lightly when it comes to your relationship with your co-packer. Remember, they make your product. Keep them happy so that they're more likely to bend over backwards for your company when you need it most.

With the relationship sorted out, let's move on.

Next I want to talk about the problems you may encounter with a co-packer and what to do about them.

What if there's a problem with my co-packer?

FOODTRUCKEMPIRE

It's never smooth sailing when you produce a food product. And problems happen with your copacker, too. Below, you'll find a couple common problems and how to solve them.

5 possible problems you may run into with your co-packer:

1. Your recipe isn't followed correctly

Yep this does happen from time to time. Mistakes happen. We're all human, right? But, this could cost your business thousands. As you read above, your co-packer may miss weigh an ingredient and not know it until it's too late. Fortunately for me, it only resulted in a few pennies of increased cost per unit (and a better product). But, if your recipe isn't followed correctly, let your co-packer know what you'd like done differently. You've done this before. They should be happy to take your suggestions.

2. You run out of ingredients

Either you overbuy or you don't have enough. It's not good either way. Too much of an ingredient means your cash is tied up. Not enough? Well, you may not be able to produce to demand. And that ultimately creates frustrated distributors, retailers, and customers. If you've got the flexibility, run out to grab ingredients at the grocery store. Yes, it increases the cost of your product, but it also saves the day. (and a potentially wasted production). Alternatively, you could simply scale back your production to align with the ingredients you have on hand.

3. You have to throw out an entire batch of product

It happens. And it's happened to my company. Unfortunately, I found out after the product was produced. I had 40 cases of bad product. But, it wasn't bad in terms of recalled ingredients. It simply wasn't the right consistency.

I don't think the mustard was heated high enough. I was out around $700. I gave the mustard away for free to family and friends. They apparently had no problem with it. But, if you have to toss product because of the lack of an ingredient, you may be able to sell it to a factory seconds store close to you so you can absorb *some*of the cost.

4. My co-packer has no kitchen time available

Sometimes you get a large purchase order and there's no available kitchen time to meet the purchase order deadline. I've been stuck in that situation many times, and it's not fun. Here's what you can do:

- See if your co-packer can switch days with someone else that's the easiest
- Fill the rest of the PO by producing in your home (if you can)

- Learn from the increased demand and schedule productions ahead of time.

Of course, this also may be a sign you need to look for a new co-packer or kitchen space. Your co-packer may not be able to meet your increased demand. If you want to grow beyond your co-packer's ability, start putting plans in place to move kitchens, or heck, even start your own kitchen.

5. Oops! I need new equipment and my co-packer doesn't want to pay

Well, the first question is how much is it? Could you finance the purchase yourself? If you can't, look at using Kickstarter to get your loyal fans to help you out, apply for a bank loan, or throw your purchase on a credit card (not recommended, but it's an option).

After the cost, ask yourself another question: do you need the equipment? Will it help you produce faster or increase the quality of your product? If you answered yes to either or both of those questions, then purchase the equipment if you can. If not, wait until you can comfortably finance it with profits from the business.

Problems happen. Just like your relationship with your significant other, you work things out. This means honest and open communication is important. Let your co-packer know you've encountered a problem and it needs to be addressed. If they're resistant to your change in process or disagreements escalate, it may be worth looking for another co-packer.

Making the switch to a new co-packer

Have you been having trouble with your current co-packer? Do you keep running into problems you wish would just never happen again?

Then maybe it's time you start the search for a new co-packer. Here's my personal story on why I switched co-packers. It comes down to three main reasons:

1. Cost

It was too expensive. My cost of goods sold was upwards of 70%. That meant no room for operating expenses like marketing and running my online store. This was mainly due to the fact we hadn't quite figured out ingredient costs and we over ordered everything. Plus, we were charged a flat day rate, driving our per unit cost through the roof. Not to mention the co-packer was an hour away. That's a lot of time and money I was wasting.

2. Size of Business

My first co-packer was simply too big for my business. I was fresh out of college, some money in the bank, and a successful energy bar company. Now, I wanted to get my mustard company off the ground. The $10,000 I had in my bank account was gone in a matter of months. Why?

Well, to make everything cost effective, we had to produce 1,000 - 1,200 units a day. Oftentimes, production spilled over into the next day, too. Every production run cost me several thousand dollars. This taught me I needed to find a smaller operation that produced closer to demand for my product. Somewhere I could produce a couple hundred units to sell at farmer's markets and a few area retailers.

3. Relationship

I just don't think we got along the way I would have liked to. I felt my interests weren't addressed and my first co-packer was focused on larger clients. Clients who co-packed thousands of units several days a week. We were small potatoes. Plus, the error that was made with the horseradish powder (see above) didn't sit right with me. I wasn't consulted when something went wrong several times. And losing trust with your co-packer is a position you never want to be in.

Your reasons to switch co-packers may be different than mine. You may have simply outgrown your co-packer's kitchen or moved your entire operation to the west coast. Whatever the reason, if you're thinking about switching to a new co-packer, make the process as smooth as possible.

How to make a smooth transition to your new co-packer

1. Tie up loose ends with your current co-packer

You may be in a contract with your co-packer. This would prevent you from leaving, unless there's a stipulation in the contract to cut ties earlier. Regardless, schedule your final production with your co-packer. Make arrangements to get ingredients and anything else in storage out and to the new location. This may mean storing things in your house or a storage locker in between productions.

It's important to note leave cordially and on good terms. Explain to your co-packer why you're leaving and that you wish them well. It's likely there aren't many co-packers to choose from in your area. Don't burn bridges!

2. Have recipes (with process) read for your new co-packer

When you move to a new co-packer, get a nondisclosure agreement signed and then send your recipes over. But, don't throw them into unknown territory. Include your scheduled process, ingredient list, and how to make the product. Does it sit overnight? Is it heated to a certain temperature? Do you want your labels put on a certain way? Your new co-packer won't know anything about this if you haven't told them.

3. New kitchen. New process.

From ingredient storage to selecting kitchen dates, and shipping purchase orders, it could all be different from your old co-packer. Be patient as you figure everything out. Your new kitchen manager should orient you to the new space, but there's still going to be a few lessons learned a couple months in. If you're accommodating and relaxed, your co-packer will be, too. And that means they'll produce high quality product for you.

You don't have to pull your hair out just to switch co-packers. It can be a quick and easy process if you follow these tips. Plus, the switch should make things easier on your cash flow (unless you're upgrading). And when you're in better shape financially you can focus on growing your business. Did someone say 'regional brand'?

Switching co-packers doesn't come without its bumps along the way. Stay patient as you work with your new kitchen manager to make the transition.

So, what's next?

What's your company look like after you've settled in with your new co-packer? Hopefully it's a lot more stress free and you're able to relax just a bit.

With that, this guide is coming to an end. Thanks for reading all the way down to the end. I really appreciate it.

Now, you're armed with all you need to know about working with co-packers. It's a tough decision to make. I hope you've learned a few things about co-packers. This is what I want you to remember as you navigate the crazy world of co-packing:

1. Find a co-packer who cares.

Someone who has as much passion as you do for your product. Who wants to follow your standard of production. And who you could call a friend.

Why do I want you to put some much time and energy into this decision?

It's not just about money. It's about your company. Your brand reputation is on the line. The second your quality standards plummet, your products aren't purchased. When your products aren't purchased, you go out of business. And that's not how you want to end your company's story, is it?

2. Have a growth mindset.

Companies who co-pack are setting themselves up for growth. Now, because you don't make your product, you can focus on sales, grow your company, and take your business to the next level.

3. Prepare for as much as possible upfront.

Things will go wrong. You will have production nightmares. You will be tight on money (After all, cash is king). And you may disagree with your co-packer. Prepare for as much as this as possible. Panicking when things go wrong won't help you. If you have an action plan to put in place when things don't go your way, you'll be much better off.

4. Know your co-packer is there to help you

They want to see you succeed. They want you to produce more product because it means you're going to spend more money with them. They'll help you plan your recipes, scale up, and produce product both of you are proud to put on grocery store shelves.
With that, let's summarize what you've learned along the way.

Here's the 10 step action plan to finding and working with your co-packer:

1. Determine if/why you need a co-packer

2. Start your co-packer search

3. Calculate costs associated with various co-packers

4. Visit several co-packers to find the right one

5. Get your recipes ready to be co-packed

6. Do a test run with your co-packer

7. Do a big production

8. Strengthen your relationship with your co-packer

 **FOODTRUCK**EMPIRE

9. Continue to evaluate if your copacker is the right fit 10. Have fun and go build your company

Pay special attention to the last one: *have fun* and go build your company. Co-packing is a business decision to honestly, make your life *easier*.It's a decision that's supposed to help you build your dream.

Jason Luedtke of Zoroco Packagingin Caldwell, Idaho, left a comment on a LinkedIn discussion about building a better relationship with your co-packer and had the following to say:

"As a glutenfree/allergen free dry good co-packer I've found that our industry is often thought of as a "necessary evil" instead of an important tool and beneficial partner. Many of our clients have come to us in a very defensive posture and with stories of dissatisfaction.

Our company is dedicated to breaking this mindset and does much in the way of transparency, communication, and customer service to try and earn the trust and loyalty of our clients.

Any solid co-packer should believe in and strive to assist the growth of their clients, it is in our best interest to have our clients grow and expand. The more we can do to see that success the better for everyone!"

Jason's right. Co-packers are partners. As I said earlier in the guide, you're practically married to your copacker. They are such an integral part of your company (they manufacture your product!) that you need to work with them to help you and help them.

Where does that leave you?

Use this guide. Read through it once or twice.

About Michael Adams

At just 25 years old, Michael Adams has been involved with three food businesses, each with their own lessons along the way. Here's a little bit about each company:

Adams' Cookie House

When Michael was 15 years old, he couldn't land a job. Eager to pay his own way to movies and hanging out with his friends, he started a cookie business out of his parent's home in Richmond, VT. Taking inspiration from Betty Crocker herself, Michael baked cookies on Friday night and sold them the next morning in front of the hair salon downtown. Surprisingly, he made a couple hundred bucks a week for a few summers. And this is what got him started in the food business.

Eddie's Energy Bars

Fast forward to senior year of high school. Michael was enrolled in a business class with a passionate entrepreneurial driven teacher who noticed Michael's potential. Eager to learn more, Michael worked directly with his teacher to learn the ropes of business. What came from working together was Eddie's Energy Bars.

Michael and his siblings competitively swam for several years. To power through their next race, they'd snack on mass made energy bars. One day after a race, Michael bit into a chocolate Powerbar. And that was the last Powerbar he ate. He was finished with eating chocolate flavored duct tape. He wanted to create his own bar.

Partnering with his Dad, Ed, of which the company was named after, they got to work deconstructing an oatmeal cookie recipe. They took out all the "bad stuff" and replaced it with good whole ingredients like apricots, yogurt, and applesauce. Two years later, they landed on the ultimate cinnamon raisin energy bar.

With a recipe in hand, Michael started to promote the bars at school events and they took off! He asked his business teacher for help writing a press release. They wrote one together in the hour before school started and sent it off to local media.

With a stint on MadeinVermont, a local TV series, Michael's small company was off to the races. He garnered press in Backpacker Magazine, Health.com, and even was listed as one of Entrepreneur Magazine's Hot 100 companies.

He created all kinds of flavors. He had loyal fans, and a growing list of local retailers. Ultimately, the fresh product and lack of fast enough inventory turns, as well as taking up his parent's weekends baking energy bars, was enough for Michael to transition out of the energy biz. But, he had to pounce on his next new idea.

Green Mountain Mustard

While the energy bars and mustard company did overlap for a few months, Green Mountain Mustard prevailed. Launched in May 2010, Green Mountain Mustard set out to be Vermont's Local Mustard. Using local eggs, butter, and maple syrup, he launched GMM with three flavors Sweet Hot, Horseradish, and Jalapeno.

After heading to the local farmer's market and selling out week after week, Michael kept creating new flavors, while making loyal fans at the same time.
Three and a half years later, Green Mountain Mustard is now known for different mustard. For celebrating mustard that isn't bright yellow. Mustard that can be served on more than a ballpark frank.

Michael currently runs this company with his parents, Jeanne and Ed, out of Richmond, VT. You can find Green Mountain Mustard in over 50 retailers across New England and at fairs and festivals throughout the northeast.